The Bible on the Question of Homosexuality

The Bible on the Question of Homosexuality

INNOCENT HIMBAZA

ADRIEN SCHENKER

JEAN-BAPTISTE EDART

Translated with an introduction by
Benedict M. Guevin, O.S.B.

The Catholic University of America Press
Washington, D.C.

Nihil Obstat:
Rev. Christopher Begg, S.T.D., Ph.D.
Censor Deputatus

Imprimatur:
Most Rev. Barry C. Knestout
Auxiliary Bishop of Washington

Archdiocese of Washington

October 25, 2011

The *nihil obstat* and *imprimatur* are official declarations
that a book or pamphlet is free of doctrinal or moral error.
There is no implication that those who have granted the
nihil obstat and the *imprimatur* agree with the content,
opinions, or statements expressed therein.

Library of Congress Cataloging-in-Publication Data
Himbaza, Innocent, 1965–
[Clarifications sur l'homosexualité dans la
Bible. English]
The Bible on the question of homosexuality /
Innocent Himbaza, Adrien Schenker, Jean-
Baptiste Edart ; translated with an introduction by Bene-
dict M. Guevin.
p. cm.
Includes bibliographical references (p.   ) and index.
ISBN 978-0-8132-1884-7 (pbk. : alk. paper)
1. Homosexuality—Biblical teaching.
I. Schenker, Adrian, 1939–   II. Edart, Jean-
Baptiste.   III. Title.
BS680.H67H5513 2012
220.8'306766—dc23   2011033131

Contents

Acknowledgments

I wish to thank James Kruggel, acquisitions editor for the Catholic University of America Press, for his hard work and diligence in shepherding this translation to its acceptance by the editorial board of the press. In a special way, I am deeply indebted to Mme. Danielle Lesage-Blais for the hours she spent reviewing my translation, for the many years of friendship, and for instilling in me a love of the French language, history, and culture.

Introduction to the English Translation

The acceptance or prohibition of same-sex relations is not an exclusively biblical or even religious concern. Such relations are known on all continents, in all cultures, and across the span of history and have been and are subject either to legal prohibition, judicial condemnation, neutrality, or acceptance.

We are concerned here with same-sex relations and the Bible. There have been a number of important studies on homosexuality and the Bible.[1] Regardless of the position one takes on the issue, the notion of writing about the topic of homosexuality in the Bible is, in fact, a bit of an anachronism. The Bible does not mention the words "homosexual" or "homosexuality." In fact, the first known use of the word "homosexual" does not appear in print until 1869 in a pam-

---

1. E.g., Daniel A. Helminiak, *What the Bible Really Says about Homosexuality: Recent Findings by Top Scholars Offer a Radical New View* (Alamo Square Distributors, 2000); Michael Vasey, *Strangers and Friends: A New Exploration of Homosexuality and the Bible* (London: Hodder and Stoughton, 1995); Donald J. Wold, *Out of Order: Homosexuality in the Bible and the Ancient Near East* (Grand Rapids, MI: Baker Books, 1998); Robert L. Brawley, ed., *Biblical Ethics and Homosexuality: Listening to Scripture* (Louisville, KY: Westminster/John Knox Press, 1996); Greg L. Bahnsen, *Homosexuality: A Biblical View* (Grand Rapids, MI: Baker Books, 1978); Dan O. Via and Robert A. Gagnon, *Homosexuality in the Bible: Two Views* (Minneapolis, MN: Fortress Press, 2003); Martii Nissinen, *Homoeroticism in the Biblical World* (Minneapolis, MN: Fortress Press, 1998); Jack Rogers, *Jesus, the Bible, and Homosexuality*, revised and expanded edition (Westminster/John Knox Press, 2009).

phlet published anonymously (later acknowledged to have been written by Karl Maria Kertbeny) arguing against Prussian anti-sodomy laws.[2] Ten years later Gustav Jager used Kertbeny's neologism in his work *Discovery of the Soul*. In 1886, Richard von Krafft-Ebing used the terms "homosexual" and "heterosexual" in his book *Psychopathia Sexualis*,[3] the first psychological approach to homosexuality as a discrete phenomenon.

Given the late appearance of the term "homosexual" in writing, would one be misdirected in exploring it in the Bible? Yes and no. Yes, because the phenomenon of a homosexual *orientation*, while certainly real, was unknown to the authors of the Bible. Certainly the Scriptures refer to same-sex relations; but they do not refer to them in quite the same way that we do today. No, because the Scriptures are seen as presenting normative and non-normative behaviors that have served as guides to moral behavior, however truly or falsely, in those religions that stem from the Abrahamic tradition.

What the Scriptures purportedly say or do not say about homosexuality is central to some of the most contentious contemporary issues: from homosexual relations *tout court*, to gay marriage, gay adoption, military service, priestly and episcopal ordinations. However anachronistic the study of the Bible and homosexuality may appear to be, it is important to deal with the issue if we are going to have a truthful and meaningful dialogue about same-sex relationships.

2. Cf. Jean-Claude Feray, "Homosexual Studies and Politics in the 19th Century: Karl Maria Kertbeny," *Journal of Homosexuality* 19:1 (1990); Karl Maria Kertbeny, *Gay History.com* at http://www.gayhistory.com/rev2/events/kertbeny.htm,

3. Cf. *Psychopathia Sexualis*, *Kino.com* at http://www.kino.com/psychopathia/history/html.

The three authors of this book are well aware of the hermeneutical difficulties that one faces when attempting to discern what the Bible says about homosexuality. They write, "In order to say something about homosexuality and the Bible, one has to clarify first what the Bible says and what goes beyond its purview. It is only after this that one can ask if the biblical teaching retains its value in this or that society." Who are these authors? What expertise do they bring to this study?

Professor Himbaza, a Protestant from the University of Fribourg, teaches Old Testament (both exegesis and theology) as well as Jewish literature from the Hellenistic and Roman periods. Author of many articles and books on various aspects of the Old Testament, Himbaza is currently working on the *Biblia Hebraica Quinta,* for which he is editing the Book of Leviticus. His task is to study the stories most often cited in discussions on homosexuality—for example, the story of Sodom and Gomorah (Genesis 19), its parallel in the story of the men of Gibeah (Judges 19), and the relationship between Jonathan and David found in 1 and 2 Samuel.

Professor Schenker is a Dominican and professor of Old Testament and, like Himbaza, also teaches at the University of Fribourg. In addition to his teaching duties, Schenker is the former president of the Theological Commission of the Swiss Bishops as well as a member of the Committee of Scholarly Editions of the *Deutschen Bibelgesellschaft* and of the *Weltbundes der Deutschen Bibelgesellchaft.* Outside of Switzerland, Schenker was a former member of the Pontifical Biblical Commission and is the coordinator of the Commission of the *Bibilia Hebraica Quinta.* He deals with the Levitical laws (Leviticus 18 and 20) and the behaviors that they prohibit, setting them within their immediate context. He is thus in a position to answer the question why the practice of homoerotic acts is forbidden by the Law of Moses.

Professor Edart teaches at the John Paul II Institute in Melbourne, Australia. Author of a number of books and articles on the New Testament, Edart has also delivered many papers worldwide. He is currently working on a liturgical translation of St. Paul's Letter to the Philippians and of 1 Corinthians 1–9 for the *Traduction Liturgique de la Bible*. In addition, he is participating in the project "The Bible and its Traditions" at the Ecole Biblique et Archéologique de Jérusalem, for which he is preparing a translation and commentary on Philippians. He focuses his attention on the writings of St. Paul regarding homosexual practices (Romans 1; 1 Corinthians 6; 1 Timothy 1). Does the New Testament teach something different from what we find in the Old Testament? How can these texts, he asks, enter into the contemporary debate?

As for the translator: I am a Benedictine monk and priest. I am a professor of Theology at Saint Anselm College, where I teach Biblical Theology and Theological Ethics, including Sexual Ethics. I hold an S.T.D. in Moral Theology from the Institut Catholique de Paris and a Ph.D. in History of Religions and Religious Anthropology from the University of Paris-Sorbonne. My principal fields of interest are Medical Ethics, Religious Anthropology, Patristics and Monastic studies. This is the second book I have translated for the Catholic University of America Press.[4] I undertook this

4. I have previously published the translation *Aquinas's Summa: Background, Structure & Reception* by Jean-Pierre Torrell (Washington, D.C.: The Catholic University of America Press, 2005). Among my many other publications, I have authored *Christian Anthropology and Sexual Ethics* (Lanham, MD: University of America Press, 2002) and have co-authored with Jozef Zalot, *Catholic Ethics in Today's World* (Winona, MN: St Mary's Press, 2008; rev. ed., Winona, MN: Anselm Academic, 2011).

translation for two reasons: first, I love French and am always looking for an interesting work to translate; second, even though I am a professor, I will always be a student. As priest, professor, and student, I have a pastoral and academic interest in this topic. I have read a number of works that assert that the Bible is essentially silent on the question of homosexuality or that, because of the claim that Jesus was a homosexual, that it is positively celebrated. I have also read books that claim that the Bible condemns homosexual behavior as being at odds with God's created order and that it can never be an expression of a biblical rule of life. Himbaza, Schenker, and Edart bring their own perspective to the debate. Each side of the debate invokes the Bible to support its position. Having been exposed to one side, I decided it was time to examine the other. What better way than to do a translation!

This book is not a moral treatise on homosexuality. Rather, it has as its aim to shed light on what the Bible has to say about the question of homosexuality. Some authors seem to place scholarship at the service of a pro-gay or anti-gay ideology; others are more scholarly, yet hard-hitting; still others at least have the appearance of disinterestedness. None of these books deals with the Bible and homosexuality in quite the same way that Himbaza, Schenker, and Edart do. Their approach is irenic, whence its appeal for me. They are scholars interested in discovering what the Bible has to say about homosexuality without taboo or prejudgment. Nor do they have recourse to personal or ecclesial interpretations. They take seriously the world from which the biblical texts emerge, and discuss the hermeneutical challenges raised by Scripture. They deal with the full range of issues raised by homosexuality in the Bible, including Jesus' own sexuality (and his relationship with the Beloved Disciple). Their conclusions are modest.

While all three authors claim to "give themselves to the text without personal or ecclesial interpretations," I am less sanguine about accepting this claim *a priori*. However much one strives to be objective, is objectivity ever really achievable? It is difficult, nay almost impossible, to divest oneself completely of one's interpretive perspective. With this caveat, I believe that they have achieved the goal of relative objectivity sincerely and insofar as this is possible.

The book is divided into three sections. In the first section, Prof. Himbaza looks at the whole range of Old Testament texts: Sodom and Gomorrah, the outrage at Gibeah (Judges 19), the relationship between Jonathan and David, and the relationship between Saul and David. In the second section, Prof. Schenker asks the question: Why did the Law of Moses forbid homosexual relations (Leviticus 18:22 and 20:13)? Among the issues he raises is the need for clear familial relationships, as well as the issue of homosexual relations within the context of the taboo against incest. He also examines, in its historical context, the issue of the death penalty for those caught in a homosexual relation and the significance of that penalty from the perspective of biblical theology. In the third and final section of the book, Prof. Edart looks at homosexuality within the New Testament. He first examines the Pauline texts (1 Corinthians 6:9–10 and 1 Timothy 1:10; Romans 1:18–32). He then examines Jesus and the healing of the centurion's slave in Luke 7:1–10; his relationship with the Beloved Disciple; Jesus' attitude toward homosexual acts; and finally, the commandment of love.

The authors' conclusion recaps their findings from the Pauline literature and from the life of Jesus. There follows a synthesis of the results of their study of the Old and New Testaments, concluding with an answer to the question: What does the Bible say about homosexuality?

Given the current controversy in the Anglican Communion regarding homosexuality, as well as the Catholic Church's position on homosexual relations, this book can be of great service. Its arguments will probably not convince either pro-gay or anti-gay ideologists. But its irenic tone, its attempt at disinterestedness, and its modest conclusions may offer readers something to ponder as we wrestle with such questions as homosexual relations, homosexual unions/marriages, practicing homosexual clergy, homosexual adoption, and gays in the military.

REV. BENEDICT M. GUEVIN, O.S.B.

The Bible on the Question
of Homosexuality

Introduction

Concerning This Work

Homosexuality is a fact of life. It has been the object of numerous publications from sociological, psychological, theological, and other perspectives. For theology, the Bible plays an important role in positions for and against homosexuality. Concerning the use of Scripture, we can ask several questions. Can we speak of homosexuality in the Bible since this term itself is recent (nineteenth century)? What does the Bible really say? How does it say it and why? This book proposes to return to the sources in order to answer these questions.

Reading the Bible today becomes more and more demanding because it reflects a society and a culture different from those of the reader. In a human society which is evolving very quickly and with rapidly changing ideas, the readers of the Bible are invited to make the necessary distinction between what the Bible teaches and what the society in which they live advocates.

The difficulty with biblical approaches is to adapt the Bible to how we live. The interpretation and contextualization of the biblical text are in themselves good things to the extent that they allow each generation to be spiritually nourished by the "word of God." Problems can arise when we want to find in the Bible answers to specific questions raised by the society in which we live. We risk making the Bible say what it does not. The interpretation can be forced so that the text is understood in a way that pleases the reader by confirming his or her point of view or by challenging another's point of view. We can also force the Bible to say something about a subject on which it is silent. This is why readers should begin with the hermeneutical presupposition that allows the text to speak for itself.

Concerning homosexuality, this hermeneutical presupposition would avoid a too benevolent (homophiliac) or too hostile (homophobic) interpretation. With respect to the Bible, the question is neither hemophiliac nor homophobic. This would be only a personal opinion. Rather, it is to understand and to interpret well the biblical text. In order to say something about homosexuality and the Bible, one must first clarify what the Bible says and what goes beyond its purview. Only after this can one ask if the biblical teaching retains its value in this or that society.

In this book, three Christian exegetes, two Catholic and one Protestant, wanted to undertake this first challenge: to examine the biblical text closely and to reread it without taboo or prejudice, in order to clarify what the Bible has to say about homosexuality. They have agreed to give themselves to the text without personal or ecclesial interpretations. This book, which is not an ethical treatise on homosexuality, shows the weight of the Bible on this question.

Outline and Content

This book is divided into three parts. These parts reflect those passages that deal with the subject of homosexuality: the stories and laws of the Old Testament, as well as the teaching of the New Testament.

Each Old Testament story has as its point of departure a concrete situation, in order to assist the reader to draw a lesson for him or herself. Innocent Himbaza examines the stories that are often cited in discussions of homosexuality such as the story of Sodom (Genesis 19), the men of Gibeah (Judges 19) as well as the love between David and Jonathan found in the book two books of Samuel. Do these stories in fact deal with homosexuality? If not, why continue to cite them? If yes, what precisely do they say?

Then, the laws of the Old Testament provide a rule of conduct, but without explaining the context from which they emerged. Adrien Schenker examines the laws concerning homosexuality in Leviticus 18 and 20. These laws are short and clear. The question then is not whether these laws forbid homosexuality or not. On the basis of a reading of these laws in their concrete context, Schenker responds to the question why the practice of homosexual love is forbidden by the law of Moses.

The position of the New Testament with respect to homosexuality flows from the legacy of the Old Testament. Does the New Testament say something different from the Old Testament? Jean-Baptiste Edart looks at the New Testament moral teaching on homosexuality, especially the texts of Saint Paul (1 Corinthians 6; Romans 1; 1 Timothy 1). He makes clear what is at stake theologically from the Apostle's position before asking in what sense the gospels can intervene in the debate on homosexuality in the Bible.

1 Old Testament Stories and Homosexuality

To speak of homosexuality in the Old Testament is not easy, because the Bible does not address the question of a sexual inclination toward members of the same sex as it is seen today today. On the other hand, homosexual behavior is known in the Bible. One can say that the Bible knows a certain kind of homosexuality. The question, then, is not to show that homosexuality is or is not known in the Old Testament. It is rather to demonstrate what is said of it. This question can be treated in the same way as other subjects dealing with sexual behavior. Homosexuality occupies only a small place in the ethical reflections of the Old Testament. Outside of a few legal texts, few stories deal with the issue of homosexual acts. In this chapter, we will first study those stories that are traditionally known as being against homosexuality. Then we will consider those that part of the current research considers to be a model of the tolerance of the Old Testament toward homosexuality.

Sodom and Gommorah

A Bad Reputation before Its Destruction

It is at the time of its settlement by the descendents of Canaan (Gen. 10:15–20) that the cities of Sodom and Gomorrah are mentioned for the first time in the Bible. Recall that before this settlement, Canaan had just been damned by his grandfather Noah (Gen. 9:24–26).[1] The names of the first descendents of Canaan, cited in Gen. 10: 15–17, correspond to populations that later will be expelled and exterminated by Israel in order that Israel may inherit the Promised Land (Ex. 3:17; 23:23; 33:2; 34:11–13; Dt. 7:2–5). Even if Lot chooses this well-irrigated region before its destruction, the text makes it clear that the inhabitants were bad and that they sinned gravely before the Lord (Gen 13:10–13). An attentive reader will have taken into account that the story already mocks the kings of that region by means of an anecdote that highlights their lack of military readiness. In fact, at the time of their flight before the coalition lead by the king of Elam, only the kings of Sodom and Gomorrah, out of the five kings of the vanquished coalition, fall into the pits of bitumen. Moreover, the spoils pillaged from Sodom and Gomorrah will be recovered by Abram (the future Abraham), the Hebrew, who was at the head of three hundred and eighteen warriors. On returning from his expedition, Abram distances himself from the king of Sodom at the same time that he draws closer to Melchisedek, the king of Salem, about whom the text says that he is also a priest of the Most High (14:17–

1. The story of the cursing of Canaan, the grandson of Noah (Gen. 9:18–27) is enigmatic. The text of verse 22 says that Ham, the son of Noah, had seen his father naked and told his brothers about it. The reading does not explain very well why it was Canaan, the grandson of Noah, who was cursed and not his father Ham. Canaan is probably introduced here because he is the ancestor of the Canaanites, a people whose country Israel would later occupy. A Jewish tradition (Talmud of Babylon, *Sanhedrin* 70a), followed by certain of our contemporaries, says that Ham had sexually abused his father and emasculated him for forbidding him to have a fourth son. This interpretation seems to have come from the late reception of this text in a specific milieu; it is not suggested by the text itself, and so we will not spend much time on it.

24). From the beginning, the Bible regards the inhabitants of Sodom and Gomorrah negatively. This attitude is probably already colored by the story of their destruction.

In Gen. 18:20–21, the Lord says that the outcry against Sodom and Gomorrah is so great and their sin so serious that he must descend to find out about it himself. In spite of this, the heavy sin of Sodom and Gomorrah is not specified. For Abraham, who intercedes before the Lord, there must surely be a few just in the region. This will be confirmed by the hospitality of Lot (19:1–5) who acts like Abraham himself (18:1–5). As things would have it, the continuation of the story shows that there were not even ten righteous in Sodom and that the only righteous one was the resident alien. The visit of the angels will confirm the outcry and will justify the measure taken by the Lord to destroy this city.

We can already see that before the story of the visit of the angels to Sodom, the inhabitants of that region were known to be great sinners against the Lord. Still, we do not know the sins of which they are guilty. The following story answers this question. Some scholars think that one should read the story found in Gen. 19 with a focus on Lot rather than on Sodom and Gomorrah. The reader would then see that the text highlights the deliverance and the grace of God.[2] For the purposes of this book, we will focus on Sodom in order to raise a societal question.

The Angels and the Destruction of Sodom

GENESIS 19:1–29 (NAB): [1] The two angels reached Sodom in the evening, as Lot was sitting at the gate of Sodom. When Lot saw them, he got up to greet them; and bowing down with his

2. See for example, P. Tonson, "Mercy without Covenant: A Literary Analysis of Genesis 19," *Journal of the Old Testament* 95 (2001): 95–116.

face to the ground, [2] he said, "Please, gentlemen, come aside into your servant's house for the night, and bathe your feet; you can get up early to continue your journey." But they replied, "No, we shall pass the night in the town square." [3] He urged them so strongly, however, that they turned aside to his place and entered his house. He prepared a meal for them, baking cakes without leaven, and they dined. [4] Before they went to bed, all the townsmen of Sodom, both young and old—all the people to the last man—closed in on the house. [5] They called to Lot and said to him, "Where are the men who came to your house tonight? Bring them out to us that we may have intimacies with them." [6] Lot went out to meet them at the entrance. When he had shut the door behind him, [7] he said, "I beg you, my brothers, not to do this wicked thing. [8] I have two daughters who have never had intercourse with men. Let me bring them out to you, and you may do to them as you please. But don't do anything to these men, for you know they have come under the shelter of my roof." [9] They replied, "Stand back! This fellow," they sneered, "came here as an immigrant, and now he dares to give orders! We'll treat you worse than them!" With that, they pressed hard against Lot, moving in closer to break down the door. [10] But his guests put out their hands, pulled Lot inside with them, and closed the door; [11] at the same time they struck the men at the entrance of the house, one and all, with such a blinding light that they were utterly unable to reach the doorway. [12] Then the angels said to Lot: "Who else belongs to you here? Your sons (sons-in-law) and your daughters and all who belong to you in the city—take them away from it! [13] We are about to destroy this place, for the outcry reaching the LORD against those in the city is so great that he has sent us to destroy it." [14] So Lot went out and spoke to his sons-in-law, who had contracted marriage with his daughters. "Get up and leave this place," he told them; "the LORD is about to destroy the city." But his sons-in-law thought he was joking. [15] As dawn was breaking, the angels urged Lot on, saying, "On your way! Take with you your wife and your two daughters who are here, or you will be swept away in the punishment of the city." [16] When he hesitated, the men, by the LORD'S mercy, seized his hand and the hands of his wife and his two daughters and led them to safety outside the city. [17] As soon as they had been brought outside, he was told: "Flee for your life! Don't look back or stop anywhere on the Plain. Get off to the hills at once, or you will be swept away." [18] "Oh, no, my lord!" replied Lot. [19] "You have already thought enough of your servant to do me the great kindness of intervening to save my life. But I cannot flee to the hills to keep the disaster from overtaking me, and so I shall die. [20] Look, this town ahead is near enough to escape to. It's only a small place. Let me flee there—it's a small place, isn't it?—that my life may be saved." [21] "Well, then," he replied, "I will also grant you the favor you now ask. I will not overthrow the town you speak of. [22] Hurry, escape there! I cannot do anything until you arrive there." That is why the town is called Zoar. [23] The sun was just rising over the earth as Lot arrived in Zoar; [24] at the same time the LORD rained down sulphurous fire upon Sodom and Gomorrah (from the LORD out of heaven). [25] He overthrew those cities and the whole Plain, together with the inhabitants of the cities and the produce of the soil. [26] But Lot's wife looked back, and she was turned into a pillar of salt. [27] Early the next morning Abraham went to the place where he had stood in the LORD'S presence. [28] As he looked down toward Sodom and Gomorrah and the whole region of the Plain, he saw dense smoke over the land rising like fumes from a furnace. [29] Thus it came to pass: when God destroyed the Cities of the Plain, he was mindful of Abraham by sending Lot away from the upheaval by which God overthrew the cities where Lot had been living.

General Overview

This text responds to the questioning of the Lord, who, according to Gen. 18:21, wanted to verify the gravity of the sin of Sodom and Gomorrah. First of all, as soon as the angels arrive in Sodom (vv. 1–3), they are well received. The hospitality of the first man they run into is at odds with the cry that had reached the Lord. This gesture, however, will not count in favor of the people of Sodom, since they themselves declare that the hospitable man is nothing but a resident alien (v. 9). In fact, in this story, Lot's presence in this story highlights the corruption of the people of Sodom.

The people of Sodom desire to "know" (*yada'*) the two men welcomed by Lot. Generally speaking, scholars recognize in this verb a sexual connotation found elsewhere in the Bible, for example, in Gen. 4:1 (the man knew his wife) or in Lk. 1:34 ("I do not know man"). On this basis, the question of homosexuality among the residents of Sodom is raised, from which comes the expression "Sodomites." It is clear that Lot's proposal to give them his two daughters accentuates the sexual connotation of their intentions. It seems to us that the context is clear to understand the text in this way.

Verse 4 makes it clear that all of the people, from the youngest to the oldest, encircled Lot's house. Now looking at the text more closely, it is difficult to imagine that all of the inhabitants of Sodom were homosexuals in the current sense of the term. In spite of the fact that the expression "all the townsmen" can include women and little children, we have to think that the redactor probably means a group of men. The main reason for this is that this mob surrounding Lot's house resembles a war expedition, something not fitting for very young children. The people of Sodom are bent on taking Lot's two visitors, if necessary by force (Gen. 19:19). Moreover, Lot's proposal to hand over his daughters (v. 8) seems to indicate that these were men. Finally, the expression "all the townspeople" is found elsewhere in the Bible to refer to a group of men (2 Sam. 6:1–2). We are dealing then with a global expression which does not seek to identify the constitutive elements of a people. It is hard to imagine that Lot's two sons-in-law, who were going to marry his daughters, were homosexuals. On the other hand, they are going to share the fate of inhabitants of Sodom because they did not listen to the word of Lot. The expression "all the townspeople" is simply a redactional note which, on the narrative level, confirms the seriousness of Sodom's sin. It explains the reason for the total destruction of Sodom: there was not the minimum of righteous necessary to spare the city (cf. Gen. 18:32).

It is interesting to note that, during the discussion with the inhabitants of Sodom, Lot finds himself outside the house (v. 7). Thus, he too was in danger of being harmed if he did not give up his visitors. Still, while he was at their mercy, he was only pushed violently away from the door. Clearly, the inhabitants of Sodom did not want to know the men because they were men, but first and foremost because they were strangers. The men of Sodom used the cover of night to give themselves over to debauchery with these unknown men. By definition, these men were at the mercy of the indigenous population.

This story confirms the outcry that had reached the Lord. The inhabitants of Sodom refused the hospitality that was offered to them by Lot, and it was not the resident alien Lot who was going to change their minds. These inhabitants were also violent and debauched, and they refused to listen to reason. Their behavior stands in contrast with Abraham's and Lot's when confronted by strangers. The experience of the two angels suffices to confirm that the sin of Sodom is very serious and justifies God's punishment. The city was burned to the ground.

The Sin of Sodom and Gomorrah
in Other Traditions

In the different allusions to Sodom and Gomorrah in the rest of the Hebrew Bible, these cities become the symbol of sin or corruption.[3] Certain texts compare the sin of Sodom and Gomorrah to the behaviors seen in Jerusalem: they proclaim their sin and do not hide it (Es. 3:9); they give themselves over to adultery, living in lies and siding with the wicked (Jer. 23:14). Others describe clearly the sin of Sodom: "proud, gluttonous, complacent in their prosperity, she and her daughters. But the hand of the distraught and the poor she does not strengthen. They have become pretentious, and have done what was abominable" (Ez. 16:49–50). A deuterocanonical writing says that the people of Sodom had shown a particularly cruel hatred towards strangers and others had not received the strangers who had just arrived (Wis. 19:13–14). According to some New Testaments passages, the people of Sodom followed the flesh with its depraved desire and showed contempt for lordship (2 Pt. 2:6–10); they engaged in prostitution and chased after beings of another nature (Jude 7). Without describing the sin of Sodom, the evangelists evoke its name with a refusal of hospitality (Mt. 10:14–15 // Lk. 10:10–12).

The extrabiblical traditions also speak about the sin of Sodom. The *Book of Jubilees* evokes the idea of filth, fornication, impurity (Jub. XVI.5); perversity, fornication, impurity, mutual corruption by fornication (Jub. XX.5). The *Testament of Levi* as well as the *Testament of Benjamin* speaks about lust (T. Levi XIV.6; T. Benjamin IX.1); the *Testament of Naphtali* speaks about changing the natural order (III.4);

3. H. Egelkraut, *Homosexualität und Schöpfungsordnung. Die Bibel gibt Antwort* (Vellmar-Kassel: Verlag Weisses Kreuz GmbH, 1993), 17–18.

the *Apocalypse of Paul* evokes rape (49b).[4] Philo of Alexandria describes the people of Sodom this way: "For, not only in their desire for women, they violated the marriages of their fellow citizens, but the men also joined themselves with other men without the active partner feeling shame for being of the same sex as the passive partner" (*De Abrahamo* 135). For Flavius Josephus, the people of Sodom "hated foreigners and did not engage in normal relations with them" (*Jewish Antiquities* I.94).[5]

Generally speaking, we can see that the reception of the story of Sodom and Gomorrah in the rest of the Hebrew Bible does not highlight a particular sin. On the other hand, in later literature (from the second century B.C.) the sin of Sodom is principally linked to the sexual behavior of its inhabitants.

Before raising the question of homosexuality, let us look at another story that is very similar to the one we have just examined.

The Infamy of Gibeah

Another Sodom

JUDGES 19:11−25 (NAB): [11] Since they were near Jebus with the day far gone, the servant said to his master, "Come, let us turn off to this city of the Jebusites and spend the night in it." [12] But his master said to him, "We will not turn off to a city of

4. For the French translation of these texts, see in the series La Pléaide La Bible, *Ecrits intertestamentaires*, published under the direction of A. Dupont-Sommer and M. Philonednko (Paris: Gallimard, 1987) and *Ecrits apocryphes chrétiens* I, published under the direction of F. Bovon and P. Geoltran (Paris: Gallimard, 1997).

5. Philo of Alexandria, *De Abrahamo*. Introduction, translation and notes by J. Gorez, Oeuvre de Philon d'Alexandrie 20 (Paris: Editions du Cerf, 1966), 78, 81; Flavius Josephus, *Les Antiquités juives*. Vol. 1, Books 1–3 (3rd ed.). Text, translation and notes by E. Nodet (Paris: Editions du Cerf, 2000) 53–54.

foreigners, who are not Israelites, but will go on to Gibeah. [13] Come," he said to his servant, "let us make for some other place, either Gibeah or Ramah, to spend the night." [14] So they continued on their way till the sun set on them when they were abreast of Gibeah of Benjamin. [15] There they turned off to enter Gibeah for the night. The man waited in the public square of the city he had entered, but no one offered them the shelter of his home for the night. [16] In the evening, however, an old man came from his work in the field; he was from the mountain region of Ephraim, though he lived among the Benjaminite townspeople of Gibeah. [17] When he noticed the traveler in the public square of the city, the old man asked where he was going, and whence he had come. [18] He said to him, "We are traveling from Bethlehem of Judah far up into the mountain region of Ephraim, where I belong. I have been to Bethlehem of Judah and am now going back home; but no one has offered us the shelter of his house. [19] We have straw and fodder for our asses, and bread and wine for the woman and myself and for our servant; there is nothing else we need." [20] "You are welcome," the old man said to him, "but let me provide for all your needs, and do not spend the night in the public square." [21] So he led them to his house and provided fodder for the asses. Then they washed their feet, and ate and drank. [22] While they were enjoying themselves, the men of the city, who were corrupt, surrounded the house and beat on the door. They said to the old man whose house it was, "Bring out your guest, that we may abuse him." [23] The owner of the house went out to them and said, "No, my brothers; do not be so wicked. Since this man is my guest, do not commit this crime. [24] *Rather let me bring out my maiden daughter or his concubine. Ravish them, or do whatever you want with them*; but against the man you must not commit this wanton crime."[6]

6. Regarding the text in italics: we have departed from the translation found in the TOB (*Traduction oecuménique de la bible*), drawing rather from the Hebrew Masoretic text. What is at stake in the translation is found under the title: "Les relectures controversées de Jg 19." In the TOB we read: "Here is my daughter who is a virgin; I will have her come out. Ravish her and do what you think is good."

[25] When the men would not listen to his host, the husband seized his concubine and thrust her outside to them. They had relations with her and abused her all night until the following dawn, when they let her go.

General Overview

This text deals with almost the same issue as Genesis 19. Even if there are some differences, the parallels between the two texts are striking.[7] This time, all of the actors belong to the people of Israel, descendents of the hospitable Abraham. The scene occurs at Gibeah, a city of Benjamin. The visitors, comparable to the angels, are the Levite and his concubine, accompanied by a servant and two donkeys. The host of the city, comparable to Lot, is an old man who is a resident alien in this city, since he is originally from Ephraim. The old man, whose name is not mentioned, has only one daughter, whereas Lot had two. The Levite says that he is returning to his home in the mountains of Ephraim; the fact that he was from the same region as the old man may have drawn him to the old man. Those who surround the house are not all the townsmen, as in the case of Sodom, but some men from the city described as wicked. This precision avoids inculpating all of the inhabitants of Gibeah.

According to the Hebrew Bible, the wicked men of the city of Gibeah are literally the "sons of Belial" (v. 22). This qualification can also be placed in parallel with the text of Genesis 13:13, which also makes it clear that the inhabitants of Sodom sinned gravely against the Lord. The term Belial underwent a significant evolution. It had the meaning of an

7. A careful reading of these texts leads us to believe that Jdg. 19 alters Gen 19. Here we agree with Lanoir. See C. Lanoir, *Femmes fatales, filles rebelles. Figures féminines dans le livre des Juges*. Actes et Recherches (Geneva: Labor et Fides, 2005) 191–98.

enemy of God (Na. 2:1). In the late literature of the pre-Christian era, found in the Qumran manuscripts, it designated an angel of darkness. In the New Testament, as well as in the literature of the same period, it denoted Satan (2 Cor. 6:15) or the Antichrist.[8] In the context of the book of Judges, it is possible that the expression "sons of Belial" simply meant the character of these people or may already insinuate the influence of the force of evil on them.

As in Genesis 19:5, the wicked men of Gibeah want to know the man. In the context of the story, the same verb "to know" (*yada'*) has a sexual connotation. We cannot say that the people wanted to become acquainted with the man. For one thing, the Levite had remained in the public square of the city, which leads us to believe that someone who was interested could have made his acquaintance. For another thing, the old man's answer, so similar to Lot's, leads us to understand the verb to mean what it means in Genesis 19. In both stories, the fact of raping a woman seems less odious than raping a man. This explains the proposal to hand over the women in place of the men. Later, in his reporting of the incident, the Levite said that the landowners of Gibeah wanted to kill him (Jug. 20:5).

Disputed Re-readings of Judges 19

Attempts at Modifying the Content

Scholars have often disputed the meaning of the request in verse 22 as well as the proposition in verse 24. Concerning verse 22, some think that in the earliest text, the men asked for the woman and not the man. For them, this story does not have homosexual overtones. They explain that it is under the influence of Genesis 19 that the text of Judges 19 has been

8. T. J. Lewis, art. "Belial" in the *Anchor Bible Dictionary* 1, pp. 654–56.

changed. Still, the proposal to change the content of the request has not been well received by modern scholars. As for verse 24, others think that it, too, has been added under the influence of the story of Sodom, and should be removed. Finally, others think that verse 24 was found in the old story but that the Levite's concubine was added later in this verse. Their proposal is to keep verse 24, taking out only the mention of the concubine. This way of understanding the text has convinced many modern scholars.[9]

We also know that in the story told by the historian Flavius Josephus (first century after Jesus Christ), the people of Gibeah wanted to take the woman, whose beauty they had noticed, and not the man. The host offered to substitute his own daughter for this woman in the name of hospitality, but these people ended up taking the woman and abusing her (*Jewish Antiquities* V. 141–147).[10] In a book of the *Biblical Antiquities*, attributed to Pseudo-Philo at the beginning of the first century after Jesus Christ, the scene occurred at Noba, northeast of Jerusalem. In this story, the perversion of the inhabitants is already well known, as it had been in Sodom. And just as in Sodom, all of the inhabitants assembled to claim the visitors. But, in an attempt to bring them to reason, the owner made them no offer of exchange. The inhabitants, acting by force, throw the man and his concubine outside before shamelessly abusing her, leaving aside the man. The same text explains that, in fact, the woman had been un-

9. On the state of the question, see D. Barthélemy, *Critique textuelle de l'Ancien Testament, I, Josué, Juges, Ruth, Samuel, Rois, Chroniques, Esdras, Néhemie, Esther.* Orbis Biblicus et Orientalis 50/1 (Fribourg: Editions Universitaires / Göttingen, Vandenhoeck & Ruprecht, 1982), 120.

10. Flavius Josephus, *Les antiquités juives*, Vol. 2, Books 4–5. Text, translation, and notes by Etienne Nodet (Paris: Editions du Cerf, 1995), 149–51. For this reading of Josephus, see L. H. Feldman, "Josephus' Portrayal (Antiquities 5.136–74) of the Benjaminites Affair of the Concubine and Its Repercussions (Judges 19–21) in *Jewish Quarterly Review* 90 (2000): 255–92.

faithful to her husband and that what happened to her was a punishment from God (*Biblical Antiquities* XLV. 1–6).

The Literary and Theological Significance
of the Change of Readings

For a long time the infamy of Gibeah has given rise to numerous contrasting interpretations. The different readings attempt to get rid of the homosexual aspect of the inhabitants, the ignoble behavior of handing over a concubine, as well as the equally immoral proposal to hand over a virgin to the mercy of the men. Even the rape of the concubine is explained theologically.

It is interesting to note that the history of the reception of the stories of Sodom and Gibeah is very different, even though they are very similar to one another in the Hebrew Bible. Theological considerations have certainly played a role in this differentiation. It appears to us that the history of the reception of the story of Gibeah attempted to attenuate the ignoble character of certain actors, probably because they are a part of the people of Israel.[11] Today's reader is therefore invited to pay close attention to the translation he or she is using, even if it is a reputable translation of the Bible. The choice of a translation influences the way in which we read the text. It should be noted that the men who asked to know the man (the Levite) and who did not want to listen to the master's offer, were finally satisfied with knowing the wife of the visitor. At the end of the story, the emphasis is on the abuse and violation of the right of hospitality.

11. See I. Himbaza, "Israël et les nations dans les relectures de Juges 19, 22–25: débats sur l'homosexualité" (forthcoming).

The Intention of the Inhabitants of Gibeah

As was the case with Genesis 19, what moved the depraved men of Gibeah to desire this man does not seem to be because he was a man, but because he was a foreigner in that region. As such, he was deprived of rights and at their mercy. This is clearly demonstrated when we consider what happened to his wife. In abusing a passing foreigner under cover of night, they probably thought that there would be no consequences to pay. Scholars note that from an anthropological perspective, the intention of the inhabitants is to show that the foreigner is subject to them; it is a question of power. This took the form of the foreigner's humiliation.[12] Recall that the servant of the Levite is not personally affected by this crime. The fact that he was not harassed by the inhabitants leads us to believe that the finality of their action was not homosexual in nature. In fact, they could have asked to know the two men (the Levite and his servant) which, moreover, would have put this story more in line with that of Genesis 19.

The Benjaminites refusal to hand over the perpetrators of this vile crime provoked a particularly bloody, punitive war. Judges 20:37, 48 makes clear that Gibeah, as well as the other cities of Benjamin, were put to the sword. This punishment is similar to that endured by Sodom and Gomorrah.[13] The smoke that rose from the city reinforces this connection (cf. Gen. 19:28).

The behavior of the inhabitants of Sodom and Gibeah is, therefore, the same; their fate is as well. Even if only a couple of men were responsible for the crime in Judges 19, the

12. K. Stone, "Gender and Homosexuality in Judges 19: Subject-Honor, Object-Shame" in *Journal for the Study of the Old Testament* 67 (1995): 87–107.

13. The biblical references also say that the neighboring cities of Sodom and Gomorrah suffered the same fate (Dt. 29:22; Jer. 49:10; Jude 7).

refusal to hand them over made all of the Benjaminites accessories.

On the narrative level, we can see a big difference between the two stories. In Genesis 19, the people of Sodom were stopped by the angels just at the moment when they began to press against Lot to push him away from the door. Even if they did not have time to carry out their plan, they made it clear what their intentions were as well as their deserved reputation as great sinners against the Lord. By contrast, the story found in Judges 19 lets the men achieve their infamous intention even if is carried out on a woman rather than on the man as was their first intention. Gibeah did not have the same evil reputation as Sodom. The redactor, therefore, takes pains to show just in what way they sinned.

Do These Stories Concern Homosexuality?

Homosexuality Is Present without Being
the Principal Subject

We saw that in the story of Genesis 19, God wanted to see for himself the reputation of the inhabitants of Sodom as great sinners, while in the story of Judges 19 the homosexuality seems circumstantial.

Neither Genesis 19 nor Judges 19 emphasizes homosexuality. That is not the purpose of the texts. On the other hand, in order to illustrate the great sinfulness of Sodom in Genesis 19 and the infamy committed in Israel in Judges 19, these stories include acts of a homosexual nature. The refusal of hospitality is expressed, among others, by the intention of performing homosexual acts on the visitors. In itself, the Hebrew expressions used, *al tare'u* (do not do this wicked thing) in Gen. 19:7 and Jdgs. 19:23, as well as *lo ta'asu devar hanevalah hazzot* (do not commit this crime), can be applied to any reprehensible act and, therefore, several contexts. Still, in the two stories, the context is clearly oriented toward sexual acts, since the host proposes to hand over the women in place of the men, seemingly as a lesser evil. "Do not commit this crime" was also the warning used in the case of Tamar, the daughter of David, before she was raped by her half-brother Amnon (2 Sam. 13:12–14). The homosexual intentions of the inhabitants of these places are part of what is reproved in these stories.[14]

One can say the same thing regarding the consideration and the right accorded to an émigré by the local population. From our perspective, it is quite judicious to say that these stories equally evoke the refusal of a complete integration of the foreigner. Even though this subject is not the primary focus of these stories, it is clearly present, as is shown by the response of the inhabitants in a direct quote (Gen. 19:9). According to these texts, the local population refuses to accept that an émigré has something to say about their customs, independently of their outrageous demand. He is tolerated, but he does not have the same status as that of the indigenous population. On this point, we can see that the exclusion does not exist only among the nations (Gen. 19), but in Israel as well (Jdgs. 19).[15] In both cases, the indigenous population closes the door to any possible peaceful solution.

As we have emphasized, others have pointed out that in

14. See P. Dickson, "Response: Does the Hebrew Bible Have Anything to Say about Homosexuality?" in *Old Testament Essays* 15 (2002): 350–67. The author responds that it has a negative attitude. He is replying to Stiebert and Walsh, who claim that the Bible says nothing about homosexuality. See Stiebert and Walsh, "Does the Hebrew Bible Have Anything to Say about Homosexuality?" in *Old Testament Essays* 14 (2001): 119–52.

15. Still Judges 21 takes up this attitude in order to show how the rest of the tribes of Israel tried to rehabilitate their brothers, the Benjaminites. Exclusion at the risk of seeing a tribe disappear is unacceptable to them.

reading Genesis 19 as a story about Lot, we can point to the theme of deliverance (cf. 2 Pt. 2:7–9). In point of fact, Lot was, at one and the same time, saved from the inhabitants of Sodom who surrounded his house and from the destruction of the city. These texts, therefore, deal with several subjects in one way or another.

A Negative Evaluation of Homosexual Practices

If we want to limit ourselves to the content of the two texts, while analyzing the question of homosexuality, we can draw three lessons.

The first is that these texts recognize the existence of homosexuality. It is present not only in foreign populations, but in Israel as well. But we should not read into these stories homosexuality as it is known today. In these texts, there is no question of persons having a marked or exclusive attraction to members of the same sex. As we have stressed, we cannot call all of the inhabitants of Sodom homosexuals. Nor can we call the wicked men of Gibeah homosexuals either, since they raped a woman at some length. In these texts, homosexuality is limited to a one-time episode. It is not understood as a desire or as a constitutive feature of the psyche.

The second teaching is that these stories condemn homosexual acts. This is an essential element of the biblical teaching on the subject. The question is not whether homosexuality existed or was known in the Old Testament, but what the biblical stories say about the *type* of homosexuality known then. We observe that in the two texts we have just looked at, the intention of committing a homosexual act is clearly condemned.[16] This condemnation is highlighted by

16. Jacob Milgrom thinks that the law regarding homosexuality (Lev. 18:22 and 20:13) concerns only Jewish males living in the holy land. He says

the genius of the redactor. The two stories are constructed in such a way that, both for the inhabitants of Sodom and and for those of Gibeah, their first avowed intention is not realized. Whereas in Genesis 19 the inhabitants of Sodom are struck with blindness before they can commit the act, in Judges 19 the rape is realized with a woman and not a man.

The third teaching concerns the seriousness of homosexual acts. In both Genesis 19 and Judges 19, the hosts qualify the intention of the inhabitants as "doing evil" or "madness/ infamy." They propose to those surrounding the house to hand over their own daughters who are still virgins rather than handing over a man. The redactors thus consider that it is less serious to rape a virgin than to rape another man. In the story of Judges 19, the proposal to hand over the wife of the Levite as well shows that, for the redactor, the rape of a man is even more serious than the violation of hospitality. The reader cannot help noticing that, in this context, the women suffer the violence and arbitrariness of the men. Nonetheless, it should be stressed that the violence done to the women is part of the unacceptable behaviors that should not be known in Israel (Gen. 34:7; Jdgs. 20:13; 2 Sam. 13:12).

Thus these texts play a pedagogical role for the reader by denouncing the reprehensible acts that they describe. Let us repeat: they insist on the protection of the passing stranger, not least because they are weak and without resources. They insist on the duty of respecting hospitality when it is offered. At the same time, they use the occasion to denounce

---

that if the homosexuality of Sodom and Gibeah had been practiced by consenting adults, they would have been expelled from the country but would not have been killed. As for us, to the extent that an act, even between consenting adults, could lead to expulsion from the country, we have to conclude that it would have been reproved. See J. Milgrom, *Leviticus 17–22: A New Translation with Introduction and Commentary.* Anchor Bible 3A (New York, London, Toronto, Sydney, Aukland: Doubleday, 2000), 1786–90.

homosexual acts and the rape of women. These acts are seen as debauchery. The same stories also stigmatize the refusal of the complete integration of the resident alien.

Jonathan and David

Several recent publications on the subject of the love between Jonathan and David affirm that it was homosexual in nature. Let us take a look at the scriptural texts in which the relationship is portrayed. In this study, we will follow a comparative approach of the texts.[17] It seems important to us to bring together certain phrases that evoke the attachment of Jonathan to David with other texts that express the attachment between two or several persons using almost the same terms. This approach will allow us to determine for ourselves the meaning that one should give to a certain word or phrase, taking into account the context as well as the philological, theological, and anthropological aspects.[18]

The first text that tells about the attachment of Jonathan to David occurs at David's return after having killed Goliath, the giant Philistine. David presents himself to Saul as "the son of Jesse your servant, the Bethlehemite" (1 Sam. 17: 55–58). This meeting is the starting point of a story with new developments.

17. For a recent bibliography of French sources, see T. Romer and L. Bonjour, *L'Homosexualité dans le Proche-Orient ancien et la Bible*. Essais bibliques 37 (Geneva: Labor et Fides, 2005).

18. M. Zehnder, "Exegetische Beobachtungen zu den David-Jonathan Geschichten" in *Biblia* 79 (1998): 153–79 follows the same line of thinking in response to an article cited by S. Shroer and T. Staubl, "Saul, David and Jonathan—The Story of a Triangle? A Contribution to the Issue of Homosexuality in the First Testament," in *Samuel and Kings: A Feminist Companion to the Bible* (Second Series), ed. A. Brenner (Sheffield: Sheffield Academic Press, 2000), 22–36.

1 *Samuel* 18:1–5

1 SAMUEL 18:1–5 (NAB): [1] By the time David finished speaking with Saul, Jonathan had become as fond of David as if his life depended on him; he loved him as he loved himself. [2] Saul laid claim to David that day and did not allow him to return to his father's house. [3] And Jonathan entered into a bond with David, because he loved him as himself. [4] Jonathan divested himself of the mantle he was wearing and gave it to David, along with his military dress, and his sword, his bow and his belt. [5] David then carried out successfully every mission on which Saul sent him. So Saul put him in charge of his soldiers, and this was agreeable to the whole army, even to Saul's own officers.

We know that, regarding the books of Samuel, questions related to the history of their redaction and to the form of the text have arisen. This passage is part of these questions in two ways, since scholars are intrigued by its presence on the one hand, and by its content on the other hand.

First of all, 1 Sam. 17:55–18:5 is not part of the short text of Samuel attested in the ancient Greek translation,the Septuagint. The history of its redaction raises a question in the mind of the reader, since a good deal of research sees it as a later addition.[19] On the other hand, this is found in the manuscript 4Q51 (4QSam^a) discovered at Qumran and which can be dated between 50 and 25 B.C. In this manuscript the only thing remaining are a few letters from verses 4 and 5.[20] It should be noted that this story is a variant one to 1 Sam. 16:14–23 since, in the two stories, David is introduced differently into

19. For a discussion of the age of one text over another, see. J. Lust, "David dans la Septante" in *Figures de David à travers la Bible*. XVIIe congrès de l'ACFEB (Lille, September 1–5, 1997), ed. L. Desrousseaux and J. Vermeylen. Lectio Divina 177 (Paris: Editions du Cerf, 1999), 243–63; S. L. MacKenzie, *Le roi David. Le Roman d'une vie*. Essais bibliques 38 (Geneva: Labor et Fides, 2006), 89–94.

20. F. M. Cross, D. W. Parry, R. J. Saley, and E. Ulrich, *Qumran Cave 4 XII 1–2 Samuel, DJD XVII* (Oxford: Clarendon Press, 2005), 4–5, 80.

Saul's inner circle.[21] 1 Sam. 16:14–23 says that David was introduced into Saul's entourage as a musician to quiet the evil spirit that tormented Saul. It should be noted that in this version it is Saul who loves (*ahav*) David (v. 21). For the reader, David and Saul are already on friendly terms even before the victory over Goliath. It is therefore surprising to see David presented to Saul for the first time in 1 Sam. 17:55–18:5.

Then, scholars note that in 1 Sam. 18:1–5, verse 2 interrupts the narrative of the love of Jonathan for David (vv. 1b, 3–4). But this narrative itself interrupts that of Saul's reaction after David has been presented (vv. 1a, 2). The scholars believe that the story has been rewritten and that, initially, it did not appear as it does now.[22] Still, these supposed modifications do not alter the recounting of the profound attachment between Jonathan and David. It seems therefore that we can take the text as it is.

Overt Words and Gestures

The story found in 1 Sam. 18:1–5 show gestures and words that express a deep attachment between Jonathan and David. David is shown as the beneficiary of steps taken by Jonathan. In the biblical context, these gestures and words are not surprising. The phrase that needs to be translated literally by "the soul of Jonathan was attached to the soul of David" recalls, in exactly the same terms, the attachment of Jacob's soul to that of his son Benjamin (Gen. 44:30–31). Jacob's deep attachment to Benjamin comes from his understanding that his other son born of Rachel, Joseph, is dead.

21. See A. F. Campbell, 1 *Samuel*, Forms of the Old Testament Literature 7 (Grand Rapids, MI /Cambridge, UK: William B. Eerdmans Publishing Company, 2003), 167–84.

22. See H. P. Smith, *A Critical and Exegetical Commentary on the Books of Samuel*, International Critical Commentary (Edinburgh: T & T Clark, 1912), 166–67.

To love (*ahav*) another as oneself (literally: "as one's soul") is a common expression. The passages 19:18 and 19:34 from the book of Leviticus command us to love our neighbor as ourselves and to love the stranger as oneself. To be more precise, literally the text of Leviticus says "as yourself" and not "as your soul." Still, "the neighbor as soul" is an expression found in Dt. 13:7 to designate an "intimate friend."[23] Scholars note that the verb "to love" in the context of an alliance has a political dimension to it, the beneficiary being considered a partner, even a superior.[24] In 1 Sam. 19:1 we find another verb used (*haphetz*, followed by the preposition *be*). According to this text, Jonathan son of Saul loved David. Literally, this means that he "took pleasure in" David. This expression is known to have an erotic dimension to it, as in Gen. 34:19. This verse concerns Shechem, who "took pleasure in" Dinah, the daughter of Jacob. The context of this entire chapter shows that Shechem fell in love with Dinah after having slept with her. The entire drama of Shechem turns on this event. In spite of this, the same expression is more often used in a larger and more neutral sense, as in the following cases: Num. 14:8: the Lord "takes pleasure in" us; he will lead us to this land. Ps. 18:20: He saved me because "he took pleasure in" me. In 1 Sam. 18:22, the servants of Saul say to David that the king "takes pleasure in" him, whence the offer to give David his daughter in marriage. A little later in 18:25, Saul has David told that he "takes no pleasure in" a wedding gift (*mohar*), but in 100 Philistine foreskins. In 2 Sam. 20:11, Joab's son asks that whoever "takes pleasure in" (that is, agrees with) Joab

23. One part of the Jewish tradition sees in the neighbor one's father because he is the closest person to you. This is not found in this verse.

24. J. A. Thompson, "The Significance of the Verb Love in the David-Jonathan Narrative in 1 Samuel," *Vetus Testamentum* XXIV (1974), 334–38.

should follow him. According to Ez. 18:32, the Lord "takes no pleasure" in the death of the sinner. The queen of Sheba declares that the Lord "took pleasure" in Solomon, that he placed him on the throne (2 Chron. 9:8), and so forth. As we can see, the expression itself is not enough to determine the meaning to be given to it. We have to consider the entire context. In the case of the love of Jonathan for David, the reader easily notices that these words explain how Jonathan impedes a political murder by standing in opposition to his father. In the context of 1 Sam. 19:1–7, nothing allows us to see an erotic connotation to "take pleasure in."

In 1 Sam. 18:4 Jonathan seems to make surprising gestures that certain people interpret as having an erotic connotation to them. He takes off his clothes and his armor in order to give them to David. By this action, he wishes David to understand his profound attachment. Still, within a larger narrative framework, we can see that David already replaces Jonathan. It is as if Jonathan were transferring to David his own prerogatives, including his right to succeed his father on the throne. Jonathan's gesture has a political dimension to it therefore, as many authors have already noted.[25] Jonathan's gesture can be understood within the framework of a treaty that he makes with David. They become so close that one becomes like another self.[26] This alliance explains

25. J. Briend, "Les figures de David en 1 S 16, 1–2 S 5, 3. Rapports entre littérature et histoire" in *Figures de David à travers la Bible,* ed. L. Desrousseaux and J. Vermeylen, 9–34, esp. 17; J. Vermeyhlen, "La maison de Saül et la maison de David" in ibid., 35–74, esp. 41–42; A. Wénin, "David roi, de Goliath à Bethsabée" in ibid., 75–112, esp. 88–89.

26. Comparing the exploits of Jonathan (1 Sam 14) with those of David (1 Sam 17), P. Lefebvre explains their attachment to each other in the fact that they find the other "endowed with the same strength and the same life which have their origin in God." *La Vie spirituelle* (2001), 199–214, esp. 203; P. Lefebvre, *Livres de Samuel et récits de résurrection. Le messie ressuscité "selon les Ecritures."* Lectio Divina (Paris: Editions du Cerf, 2004) 347–64, esp. 348.

why Jonathan will systematically take David's side against his father. From the beginning, the love that Jonathan has for David has an important theological and narrative significance. No one was better placed to know the intentions of the king and to interest himself in the royal succession than Jonathan. The stories of the friendship between Jonathan and David show a very close alliance, even to the point of one identifying with the other. This development ends with the second replacing the first.[27] This, in any case, is the direction that their story takes, since in 1 Sam. 23:17 Jonathan declares to David: "It is you who will reign over Israel. As for me, I will serve you."

What Part Does Homosexuality Play?

Ought we to see in Jonathan's gesture of giving his clothes and armor to David a sexual connotation? It seems so if we place this passage alongside Ezekiel 16. This chapter tells of Jerusalem's infidelity to the Lord using the image of a young woman abandoned from birth and taken in by a passer-by (the Lord). He takes care of her and marries her, but she abandons him in order to offer herself to any passer-by. Verse 8 of this chapter says: "I passed by you and saw that you were now old enough for love. So I spread the corner of my cloak over you to cover your nakedness; I swore an oath to you and entered into a covenant with you; you became mine, says the Lord God" (NAB). In this context, covering a woman with the corner of one's cloak (literally: spreading one's wings over

27. D. Jobling, *The Sense of Biblical Narrative: Three Structural Analyses in the Old Testament* (1 Samuel 13–31, Numbers 11–12, 1 Kings 17–18) (Sheffield: Journal for the Study of the Old Testament, 1978), 11–25. We do not believe that the behavior of Jonathan makes him David's "woman," as Y. Peleg has written in "Love at First Sight? David, Jonathan and the Biblical Politics of Gender," *Journal for the Study of the Old Testament* 30 (2005) 171–89. For us the whole business is political, not sexual.

her) means to marry her. Ruth, the Moabitess, asked Boaz to marry her using exactly the same expressions: "Marry your servant," literally: "Spread the corner of your cloak over me" (Ruth 3:9) (NAB). In the Jewish tradition (Midrash *Genesis Rabba* LXXXVII, 4), Rabbi Samuel ben Nahman (third century B.C.), having placed Ruth's request to Boaz alongside the demand made by the wife of Potiphar to Joseph ("lie with me," Gen. 39:7), observes that the two women make the same request, but that the second speaks like an animal.

The gesture of the passer-by in Ezekiel 16, tied up with the notion of oath and covenant, has clearly the meaning of marriage. Now, the two elements, the gesture with the cloak and the notion of covenant can be found in the story of Jonathan and David. Nonetheless, if we place together the gestures of Ez. 16:8 and those of 1 Sam. 18:3–4, their respective contexts are clearly very different. It seems that in the kind of approach that compares different texts, context plays a crucial role in interpreting them.

First of all, let us note that the verb to divest (*pashat*) used in 1 Sam. 18:4 is the same verb as the one used in Gen. 37:23 where Joseph is stripped of his cloak by his brothers. The difference is that in the case of Jonathan, it is he who strips himself.[28] Jonathan divests himself of his clothing, not with the aim of showing himself naked in front of David, but to give the clothing to him. The fact of giving one's clothing and armor to another is a well-known gesture. For example, when preparations were made to confront Goliath, Saul himself clothed David in his own clothing and armor (1 Sam. 17:38–39). On other occasions, the exchange of armor is likewise known. Homer (*Iliad* VI, 230) evokes the ex-

28. Philippians 2:7 uses the same image to speak about Jesus's approach toward humanity (compare 2 Cor. 8:9).

change of arms between Glaucos and Diomedes as a way of sealing a deep friendship. It seems to us that, in this story, Jonathan's actions are to be understood as another one of these gestures that expresses either an attachment or a transfer of the signs of strength or power. Nothing in this scene permits us to see an erotic connotation, which could have been expressed in other ways such as "to show oneself" or "to show one's sexual organ" to someone else (Ez. 16:36), to spread one's legs (Ez. 16:25), and so forth. An erotic context speaks about the body that one uncovers rather than clothing that one takes off.

We see in the rest of the story of Jonathan and David how, on several occasions, the two "brothers" recall their already concluded alliance or seal their alliance again before the Lord and swear mutual fidelity to each other (20:8, 14–17; 23:16–18). We know, from passages in Deuteronomy 29, that a strong alliance binds the Lord to his people.

1 *Samuel* 20:30–31

1 SAMUEL 20:30–31 (NAB): [30] But Saul was extremely angry with Jonathan and said to him: "Son of a rebellious woman, do I not know that, to your own shame and to the disclosure of your mother's shame, you are the companion of Jesse's son? [31] Why, as long as the son of Jesse lives upon the earth, you cannot make good your claim to the kingship! So send for him, and bring him to me, for he is doomed."

The incident between Saul and Jonathan occurred on the second day after the new moon, while the feast was in full swing. This incident is the logical consequence of the succession of Saul's failed attempts to kill David in order to get rid of him. Saul had first been persuaded by Jonathan to renounce his plan to kill David (19:2–7); he failed in his attempt to nail David to the wall with his spear (19:8–10); he was deceived by his daughter Michal (19:11–17); and he was led into the circle of prophets at Ramah while in pursuit of David (19:18–24). Moreover, during the first two days of the new moon, David did not present himself at the table of the king (20:24–27). The straw that broke the camel's back was that it was Jonathan himself who had given him permission to leave (20:28–29). Saul's words in 20:30–31 are an ugly insult from a man frustrated and out of control of events. He vents his anger on his son who, apparently, had not understood the political risks of allying himself with David. The story makes it clear that Saul had sensed the danger since 1 Sam. 18:7–9, when the women praised David more than himself.

Saul's insult has been understood differently throughout the ages. According to the old Greek translation from the Septuagint, Saul calls Jonathan a "son of whores," the expression being in the plural. One of the most ancient manuscripts from Qumran, 4QSam[b] (4Q52), dating from the middle of the third century B.C., is in harmony with this reading from the Septuagint. Scholars nevertheless believe that there was confusion in how the Hebrew text was read.[29] The expressions used in this insult are found in Judith 16:12, following the text of the Septuagint, to indicate a person of no account: "The sons of slave girls pierced them through; the supposed sons of rebel mothers cut them down" (NAB).

The reader's first impression is that Saul's insult has to do with Jonathan's mother, since it is she who is denigrated. The denigration of an ancestor is well known in other places in the Bible, for example, at Ezekiel 16:3, 45 where the mother and father of Jerusalem are respectively called a

29. F. M. Cross, D. W. Parry, R. J. Saley, and E. Ulrich, *Qumran Cave 4 XII 1–2 Samuel*, 232–33.

Hittite and an Amorite. This designation wants to show that "the people of God," represented by Jerusalem, is no better than the surrounding nations. We know that for a part of the Jewish tradition (Mishna, *Megillah* IV, 10), these verses form part of passages that are neither read nor translated in the synagogue. This attitude can probably be explained by the fact that these verses are seen as an affront (a kind of insult) to the people of Jerusalem that one would rather not advertise.

Let us not deceive ourselves: this kind of insult of someone's mother is not limited to the East or to ancient times. It is known everywhere, even today.[30] On the level of cultural anthropology, we know that insults directed to the mother and especially to the sex of the person who is insulted injure the most.[31] Note that these insults are directed to men and not to women. A Jewish tradition says: "Achaz permitted consanguineous marriages; Mannaseh raped his sister, and Amon his mother . . ." (Talmud of Bablyon, *Sanhedrin* 103b). The actions of these kings are unknown in the Bible. We could almost speak of a calumny whose purpose is to make them out to be worse than they were. This tradition wanted to show that impiety increased each time a new, impious king came to the throne. It should be noted that, in this exaggeration, the infamy committed against the mother is considered to be the most grave. In fact, the mother is herself the source of life, since it is she who gives birth. The person insulted is thus denigrated and dishonored in his essence itself, since the insult calls to mind the place by which he

30. P. Dhorme, *Les livres de Samuel.* Etudes bibliques (Paris: Gabalda, 1910), 187.

31. For countries where the insult is part of the art of oration, in which the lower classes and particularly the young shepherds excel, poetic insults centered on (the sex of) the mother are the most dreaded.

came into the world. Another tradition reports that to the one was reading (publicly) before Rabbi Eliezer "Make known to Jerusalem her abominations," he replied: "Rather than looking at the abominations of Jerusalem, go look at those of your mother" (Talmud of Babylon, *Megillah* 25b). The fact that one is publicly insulted makes the denigration and dishonor all the worse. This is what we have in the case of Jonathan.[32]

Some current research has interpreted this insult in the sense that Saul wanted it understood that he was aware of the homosexual relation between Jonathan and David. Still, the analysis of this insult has shown us that nothing obliges us to go in that direction. Even supposing that Saul had discovered a homosexual relation between Jonathan and David, we would have supplemental proof that homosexuality was rejected by Saul and very probably by the rest of society.

1 *Samuel* 20:40–21:1

> 1 SAMUEL 20:40–21:1 (NAB): [40] Then Jonathan gave his weapons to this boy of his and said to him, "Go, take them to the city." [41] When the boy had left, David rose from beside the mound and prostrated himself on the ground three times before Jonathan in homage. They kissed each other and wept aloud together. [42] At length Jonathan said to David, "Go in peace, in keeping with what we two have sworn by the name of the LORD: 'The LORD shall be between you and me, and between your posterity and mine forever.'" Then David departed on his way, while Jonathan went back into the city.

This meeting between Jonathan and David was held the day after the episode of the meal of the new moon. Scholars observe that the episode is difficult to understand at this

---

32. G. Stansell, "Honor and Shame in the David Narratives," in *Was ist der Mensch...? Beiträge zur Anthropologie des Alten Testaments. Hans Walter Wolff aum 80. Geburtstag,* ed. F. Crüsemann, C. Hardmeier, and R. Kessler (Munich: Kaiser Verlag, 1992), 94–114.

point in the story. In fact, while the story of the arrows was destined to make David understand what he had to do without arousing Saul's suspicions, here David leaves his hiding place and spends a few moments with Jonathan, apparently without being in a hurry.[33] Certain gestures of the two friends should be looked at closely in the context of what we have been discussing. Verse 41 says that David prostrated himself before Jonathan and that the two kissed and wept aloud together. The Hebrew verb *nisheq*, used to speak about the kiss, means "to give a kiss." At first glance, it would be obvious to conclude that the two men whom we know to love one another are giving each other a kiss, which could be an erotic gesture. For this understanding, we could appeal to the Song of Songs 1:2 and 8:1, where the same verb is also used in an erotic sense. On the other hand, as we have already highlighted in other instances, we have to examine the context closely.

Let us first of all recall that we are at the moment when the two friends are going to separate because the situation has become too dangerous for David. Therefore we are in the context of a leave taking. We know of a similar scene in the New Testament when Paul is taking leave of the elders in Ephesus. They cry and hug Paul warmly and kiss him (Acts 20:36–38).[34] The gestures of prostrating oneself before someone and hugging him, that is, giving him a kiss, are also known in the Old Testament when Moses and his father-in-law greet one another. Exodus 18:7 says: "Moses went out to meet his father-in-law, bowed down before him,

33. P. K. McCarter, *I Samuel. A New Translation with Introduction and Commentary*, Anchor Bible 8 (New York, London, Toronto, Sydney, Aukland: Doubleday, 1980), 343.

34. Paul also recommends to the Romans and Corinthians that they greet each other with a holy kiss (Rom 16:16; 1 Cor 16:20).

and kissed him. Having greeted each other, they went into the tent" (NAB). Today's reader will see erotic gestures or, in any case, suggestive gestures in witnessing two men kissing each other and entering into the tent. The comparison between the two scenes shows that Jethro and Moses go even farther than Jonathan and David. And yet, we do not say that Jethro and Moses are homosexuals. Gestures of kissing and weeping are seen in the story of Joseph and his brothers when they were reunited in Egypt. Genesis 45:14–15 says: "[14] . . . he flung himself on the neck of his brother Benjamin and wept, and Benjamin wept in his arms. [15] Joseph then kissed all his brothers, crying over each of them; and only then were his brothers able to talk with him" (NAB). These examples lead us to think that there is nothing erotic in the leave taking of Jonathan and David.

All of these cases show that in the biblical context of the Old and New Testaments, there are several gestures used when people meet through which one should not necessarily see a sexual connotation. One attaches oneself sentimentally to another; one gives clothing or arms to the other; one cries on the neck of the other; they love each other deeply and embrace (kissing each other), and so forth. These gestures can be used between parents and children (Jacob and Benjamin), between brothers (Joseph and his brothers), between father-in-law and son-in-law (Jethro and Moses), between close friends (Jonathan and David), between warriors (Saul and David; Jonathan and David), and between brothers and sisters of the faith (Paul and the Ephesians). These gestures, which are common and normal for people who feel close to each other, risk being misinterpreted by the modern reader who comes from a different culture.[35] They should

35. See also the observations of S. L. MacKenzie, *Le roi David*, 95–97.

not be confused with erotic gestures or homosexual gestures when done between two people of the same sex.

Why Do We Not Speak of a Homosexual Relationship between Saul and David?

If we wanted to pursue further the question of homosexual relations, we would see them first between Saul and David before seeing them between Jonathan and David. Saul enacts gestures of goodwill toward David before everyone. Jonathan only follows up on them. One could almost speak of a tragic love triangle. In fact, without considering the two superimposed stories, which also explains the doublets in them, it would seem that Saul and Jonathan rival each other in their love for David. Saul becomes a point of discord between the two lovers. Saul has the advantage of power, since he is the king. He can retain David or can grant him favors by naming him his shield-bearer, et cetera. For his part, Jonathan has the advantage of youth, since he is a young prince and more or less David's contemporary. Likewise, Jonathan can give his armor to David and, more easily than his father, who is taken up with affairs of state, he can meet alone with David. Saul, who was the first to throw himself into the adventure is, in the end, supplanted by Jonathan, who became closer to David than Saul was. This explains why Saul goes after them.

The table on the next page shows the parallels between Saul's and Jonathan's pursuits of David. It shows that the gestures of Jonathan are the same as those of his father. It is also interesting to note that, on the narrative level, each gesture of Jonathan follows that of Saul. The only element unique to Jonathan and David are the embraces and the leave takings, of which 1 Sam. 20:40–21:1 is a repetition. In

16:21: David goes to Saul and places himself at his service (lit.: stood before him). Saul is taken with David (lit.: he loved him a lot) and David becomes his aide.	18:1: Now, as soon as David had finished speaking with Saul, Jonathan became attached to David (lit.: Jonathan's soul was attached to David's soul).
16:22: . . . because he cares for him (lit.: he found favor in my eyes).	20:3: . . . I am pleased with you (lit.: I found favor in your eyes).
18:2: That day, Saul retained David and did not let him return to his father.	18:3: Then Jonathan made an alliance with David because he loved him as he loved himself (cf. 20:17).
17:38–39: Saul dressed David in his own clothes, put on his head a helmet of bronze, and placed his chain mail on him. [39] David also girded on Saul's sword over his tunic . . .	18:4: Jonathan took off the cloak he had been wearing and gave it to David as well as his military dress and even his sword, his bow, and his belt.
18:22: The king wishes you well (lit.: the king was pleased with him).	19:1: And Jonathan, son of Saul, was very fond of David (lit.: was well pleased with David).

the context of David's rise to power, this comparative view shows that the young shepherd and valiant warrior replaces successively Saul and Jonathan.[36]

To return to the question posed in the title of this section: we must answer that the text is not speaking about a homosexual relationship between Saul and David, simply because none exists. It seems to us that, in light of the parallels we have just laid out, it goes without saying that the same answer must be given regarding the relationship between Jonathan and David.

36. For Wenin, Goliath's death inaugurates David's reign. Cf. "David roi, de Goliath à Bethsabée," 76.

2 *Samuel* 1:26

"I grieve for you, Jonathan my brother! Most dear have you been to me; More precious have I held love for you than love for women." The context of this text is mourning. The plaint of David in 2 Samuel 1 evokes his attachment to Jonathan, but also to Saul. He calls them "beloved" and "charming" (vv. 23, 26). This text also raises questions for scholars. On the one hand, they observe that we are "in the presence of a sophisticated composition and that it would be hazardous to consider it as the spontaneous words from the lips of David." On the other hand, they see in it something very personal, a deep feeling, especially when the text concerns Jonathan.[37]

Verse 26 speaks about David's love for Jonathan: a love that is greater than that for women. A part of the Latin tradition of the Vulgate adds this to the text: "as a mother loves her only son, so have I loved you." As for the ancient Armenian translation of the Targum, the love of Jonathan for David was more than the love of two women. These rereadings show that this phrase drew the attention of its readers who wished to explain it. It would not be surprising that these witnesses to the ancient reception of this text wanted to avoid an understanding that could be misinterpreted as erotic in nature.

Verse 26 of 2 Samuel 1 has been used, particularly by certain scholars, as the basis for affirming a homosexual relationship between Jonathan and David.[38] At the very least, they say, the comparison between the love of Jonathan and that of women does not exclude an erotic connotation. We can obviously suppose that the love of Jonathan and that of

37. A. Cacquot and P. de Robert, *Les livres de Samuel*, 371.
38. Cf. T. Horner, *Jonathan Loved David: Homosexuality in Biblical Times* (Philadelphia: Westminster Press, 1978).

women are of the same nature, since they are compared. Still, we should not forget the poetic and, therefore, symbolic character of the text. David could have evoked the attachment between the two without a sexual undertone. The love of women mentioned can be that of the love of a wife for her husband, or a mother for her child. The word "love" (*ahavah*) used here is quite common. It is not limited to conjugal love (Hosea 3:1) but can also refer to God's love for his people (Es. 63:9, Jer. 11:4, 31:3) and vice versa (Dt. 6:5); the love of one's country (a region), of a slave for his master (Ex. 21:5), of the people of God for the stranger (Lv. 19:34), and so forth.[39]

It has to be recognized that the context of mourning does not allow us to exclude some kind of expression of love. As often happens after a death, tongues loosen and anything is possible. We believe therefore that we should rely on what we know about life and the relationship between Jonathan and David to determine whether or not David is referring to an erotic attachment to Jonathan. Now, none of the contexts that we have examined point toward an erotic relationship between the two.

Having examined these texts, we are left with this question: On what basis do some scholars affirm a homosexual relationship between Jonathan and David? Nissinen writes that ultimately the Bible does not answer the question as to whether or not they had a homosexual relationship.[40] As for us, we believe that we have shown that the isolated gestures

39. M. H. Pope, "Homosexuality" in *International Dictionary of the Bible, Supplement*, 415–17. A. A. Anderson, 2 *Samuel*, World Biblical Commentary 11 (Dallas: Word Books, Publisher, 1989), 19; T. Bosman, "A Critical Review of the Translation of the Hebrew lexeme אהב" *Old Testament Essays* 18 (2005): 22–34.

40. M. Nissinen, "Die Liebe von David und Jonathan als Frage der modernen Exegese," *Biblica* 80 (1999): 250–63.

that might be interpreted as erotic are not in fact so, when seen in their actual biblical context.

Of all of the texts on Jonathan and David, there is absolutely nothing that inclines us to see in their relationship a homosexual connotation. This type of relationship is neither clearly expressed nor implicitly suggested, and, we believe, it should not even be considered as doing so. It appears to us that readers should not have recourse to these texts in order to speak of a biblical tolerance of homosexuality.

Conclusion

Sodom and Gibeah: Two Sisters

The story about Sodom found in Genesis 19 emphasizes the generalized corruption of the inhabitants of this city in order to explain the reasons for its destruction. At the same time, the question of theodicy is raised. Is it judicious to destroy the entire city at the risk of killing the just with the unjust? The story responds that the just will ultimately be saved while the unjust will die. In fact, apart from the foreigner Lot and his household, the entire city is sinful. In order to illustrate the sin of the residents of Sodom more concretely, the story highlights the refusal of hospitality. This refusal is expressed by a violation of the home, the intention of committing an act of a homosexual nature on a stranger, apparently to make him submit, and finally the refusal to listen to the counsel of the foreigner and, therefore, the refusal to integrate him completely into the community.

The story in Judges 19 on Gibeah says practically the same thing. The story wishes to illustrate that Israel, or at least a part of the people, was not better than the inhabitants of Sodom. The same refusal of hospitality, the same homosexual intentions, the same refusal to integrate the resident alien completely into the community, all are found in Israel as they are found among the nations. The story in Judges 19 adds the rape of the woman and murder to the acts committed in Israel. Even though these acts can be considered as an expression of or as constitutive elements in the refusal of hospitality, they are nonetheless singled out and condemned.

If we want to stop at homosexuality, while keeping in mind the proper intention of these two texts, we could say that homosexual behavior is part of what constitutes the sins of the inhabitants of Sodom as well as those of the men of Gibeah. It can also be said that the two texts condemn this kind of behavior. To affirm that these texts say nothing about homosexual behavior seems to us to be an ideological interpretation.

Henceforth, it is now up to the reader of today to decide what to do with these texts. The reader can accept or reject them, but he or she should not twist them. If one accepts them, then two outcomes are possible: either to use them as a value judgment on homosexuality; or to limit their importance by showing the difference between that society and ours. In this case, the reader can emphasize that the stories of Genesis 19 and Judges 19 denounce the violent nature of the intention of the inhabitants of Sodom and Gibeah, whereas in today's world homosexuality is seen in the context of mutual consent. On this precise point, the stories have nothing to say. In order to know if the Bible says something about homosexual relations between two consenting persons, the reader will turn to other texts of the Old Testament, such as the legal texts found in Leviticus, or, in the New Testament, Paul's letters.

Jonathan and David: Two Brothers

In the context of today's society and regarding the subject of homosexuality, the stories of the books of Samuel are more subtle than those of the Pentateuch. They, indeed, show a profound love between two men. Now, if we compare the words and gestures used to describe this love with those that are used in an erotic context, we can certainly be lead to think that these two men were homosexuals.[41] On the other hand (and this constitutes the richness of biblical language), the same words and gestures are used and well known within a larger context and are absolutely neutral. No word, no gesture describing the love between Jonathan and David is limited to an erotic context, nor absent from common and neutral language. We have shown several examples of this. Today's reader must come to understand in what sense their love for each other is to be interpreted. We insisted on the fact that, in the case where an isolated word could have several meanings, the context determines the sense to be retained. On a philological level, that process must predominate. Now, in the case of Jonathan and David, the context is political and theological. Of all of the texts we looked at, none could be found in an erotic context. This is why we concluded that the stories that speak of the love between Jonathan and David are not examples of a tolerance of homosexuality in the Bible. For us, these stories do not deal with this subject. In using the stories of Jonathan and David to speak one way or another about homosexuality seems to us to force the texts.

41. T. R. Koch finds several other supposedly homosexual-type acts in the Bible: "Cruising as Methodology: Homoeroticism and the Scriptures," in *Queer Commentary and the Hebrew Bible, Journal for the Study of the Old Testament Supplement* 334, ed. K. Stone (Sheffield: Sheffield Academic Press, 2001), 169–80.

Again, if today's reader wishes to speak about toleration and a just attitude toward homosexuals, he or she should have recourse to other biblical texts. For instance, we could cite examples of love for others (Lev. 19:17–18, Col. 3:12–14), those which invite us to leave judgment to God (Ps. 75:8), or not to judge others lest we be judged (Lk. 6:37), to use kindness (Gal. 6:1–10), and so forth.

Why Does the Mosaic Law Forbid the Practice of Homosexual Love (Leviticus 18 and 20)?

The Reasons for and the Importance of a Biblical Rule of Life

What Foundation?

When a rule of life goes to the heart of strong and elemental human needs, it had better have strong foundations. Without them, the rule will never stand up to these needs. It will be rejected, for it will be experienced as alienating, since it seems to destroy human happiness, which is the fruit of a fulfilled need. In the name of what should one renounce a fulfillment that harms no one?

Today, persons with a homosexual orientation are not willing to submit to an ethic or an institution from the outside that forbids this kind of love which seems natural to them. By what right should one refuse them the fulfillment and happiness that comes from a love that is part of who they are? Indeed, the mutual love of adult persons who freely choose each other and are attracted to each other is experienced as one of the greatest goods that can be experienced in this life. To limit this to love between a man and a woman, and to exclude this love for persons of the same sex, would deprive a great number of human beings, attracted to the same sex, of the fulfilling experience of love expressed sexually. Consequently, one can understand that the reasons given to justify discrimination between one form of sexual love that is accepted and another that would be forbidden have to be equal to what they forbid. Without this equality, these reasons will seem as something foreign imposed from without.

Now in order to be strong, a reason must be obvious. It must be understood in the light of reason. We ask for arguments that are well founded. It is here that the rubber hits the road when one turns to the Bible. In the Torah, that is, the "Divine Law," in the book of Leviticus, the Bible does indeed forbid sexual union between two men. It does so in two places, Lev. 18:22 and 20:13.

Lev. 18:22 reads as follows: "You shall not lie with a male as with a woman; such a thing is an abomination" (NAB).

In Lev. 20:13 we read: "If a man lies with a male as with a woman, both of them shall be put to death for their abominable deed; they have forfeited their lives" (NAB).

But in these two places the prohibition is not founded on reasons. It is stated, but it is justified only by the qualification of this sexual act as an "abomination." This expression qualifies an act or a thing as being incompatible with God.[1] But why sexual relations between two men are intolerable in God's presence is not explained. Since one cannot presuppose that a rule of behavior as important as this would have accidently entered into Israelite ethics and into the Bible, it must be founded on motives that explain it. The place where

1. A. Lacroque, "Abomination," in *Dictionnaire encyclopédique de la Bible*, 3rd ed., revised, expanded and published under the direction of Centre Informatique de la Bible, Abbaye de Maredsous (Turnhout: Brepols, 2002), 7–8.

the prohibition is found in the Old Testament is central: for Leviticus 18 and 20 are part of the Torah, the "Law" which contains conditions regarding all of human life lived in conformity with God's will.

Three Proposed Explanations

The explication of the reasons and content implicit in the texts is the proper task of the exegete. How does the exegete account for the prohibition of sexual relations between two men? This exegesis proposes three principal explanations.

The Specific Difference between Israel and Other People

Perhaps the best known and the most often cited explanation is that of the difference between Israel and other people. This is based on the passages that surround Leviticus 19 and 20. In Lev. 18:3–4 the introduction to the commandments that follow highlights the distinction between Israel and other people:

> LEVITICUS 18:3–4 (NAB): [3] You shall not do as they do in the land of Egypt, where you once lived, nor shall you do as they do in the land of Canaan, where I am bringing you; do not conform to their customs. [4] My decrees you shall carry out, and my statutes you shall take care to follow. I, the LORD, am your God.

This passage is the redactional introduction to Lev. 18:6–23. We should probably distinguish it from the redactional conclusions found in Lev. 18:24–30 and 20:22–24.[2] As we shall see later, these passages implicate the entire Penta-

2. Cf. A. Schenker, "What Connects the Incest Prohibitions Listed in Lv 18 and 20?" in *The Book of Leviticus. Composition and Reception*, ed. R. Rendtorff and R. A. Kugler, FIOTL 3, VT.S 93 (Leiden-Boston: Brill, 2003), 162–85,

teuch since they implicitly presuppose the promise of the land made by God to the patriarchs and the loss of the land by the indigenous populations for the benefit of Israel. The prologue of Lev. 18:2–5, on the other hand, presents the people in the desert with a choice: they must choose between, on the one hand, the way of life of Egypt which Israel has just left and that of the inhabitants of the Promised Land toward which they are moving, or, on the other hand, God's way of life. In choosing that latter, they choose life, verse 5. The choice that Israel must make on the threshold of the Promised Land, between its God and the other gods and between life and death, is a theme of Deuteronomy (Dt. 26:16–19; 30:15–20, cf. Joshua 24). The prologue of Lev. 18:2–5 thus explains the commandments that will follow in Lev. 18–20 as the *distinctive* behavior of the Israelites in the midst of all the nations of the earth. As a matter of fact, Deuteronomy likes to explain the Law of Israel as the distinctive mark of this people. Israel must fulfill it by her concrete practice of the commandments (Dt. 4:1–9).

At the end of Leviticus 20, the difference between Israel and the other peoples is reaffirmed in the conclusion which belongs to the redactional whole of Lev. 18:24–30; Lev. 20:22–24:

LEVITICUS 20:22–24(NAB): [22] Be careful to observe all my statutes and all my decrees; otherwise the land where I am bringing you to dwell will vomit you out. [23] Do not conform, therefore, to the customs of the nations whom I am driving out

---

and especially for the redactional passages of Lev. 18:2–5; 18:24–30; 20:6–8; 20:22–26: pp. 174–80. For all questions regarding redaction and content cf. J. Milgrom, *Leviticus 17–20. A New Translation with Introduction and Commentary*, Anchor Bible 3A (New York–London: The Anchor Bible–Doubleday, 2000). This commentary is the richest on issues concerning Leviticus 18 and 20.

of your way, because all these things that they have done have
filled me with disgust for them. [24] But to you I have said: Their
land shall be your possession, a land flowing with milk and hon-
ey. I am giving it to you as your own, I, the LORD, your God, who
have set you apart from the other nations.

Israel is set apart from these nations, for it is consecrated
to the Lord. This is why she must distinguish herself from
their practices. Among these practices is also found sexual
relations between men, according to Leviticus 18 and 20.[3]

The argument of the necessary distinction of Israel from
the other peoples is a historical argument and, as a consequence, relative, from the point of view of the theological relationship between the Jewish faith and the Christian faith.
This means, in effect, that a particular historical condition
desired this interpretation. But this historical condition having disappeared, the prohibition itself has lost its *raison
d'être*. Notably, modern Christian readers have no reason to
distinguish themselves from early peoples such as the Canaanites. This distinction had as its aim to keep Israel from
mixing with these nations thereby losing its own identity.
This is why this explanation of the distinctiveness of Israel
logically leads to the abandonment of the prohibition of sexual relations between men, since these relations were tied
to a particular historical situation that does not exist for the
non-Israelites.

To Protect Fertility, to Ensure a Progeny

Another explanation comes from the value of fertility that
was very highly esteemed among ancient people.[4] Since ho-

3. Representative of this interpretation, for example, is M. Douglas, "Justice as the Cornerstone: An Interpretation of Leviticus 18–20" in *Interpretation* 53 (1999): 345–47.
4. J. Milgrom, *Leviticus 17–20*, pp. 1567–68.

mosexual relations are not fertile, they are forbidden just as the Mosaic Law, in the same chapters, forbids intercourse between a man and a woman during menses. As a matter of fact, we can explain this prohibition by the desire to avoid useless fertilization, washed away in the menstrual flow. Clearly, conditions have changed between the period of ancient Israel with its great esteem for fertile carnal relations and the period of the modern West. This is why many of our contemporaries do not understand the reason for the Catholic Church's ethical requirement that sexual relations must be open to the possibility of bringing forth new life.

To Protect the Peace in an Extended Family, to Ensure the Safety of Each One of Its Members

A third explanation comes from a context in which is found the prohibition of homosexual relations. Just as certain sexual relations are forbidden between close relatives, so also are homosexual relations forbidden. Incestuous relations profoundly disturb family harmony and, as a consequence, the interior peace of a family, because they place the family members in a contradictory situation. On the one hand, they have their place in the family system since they are father or mother, son or daughter, brother or sister, etc., and, on the other hand, they find themselves the object of desire. What role then must they play? In invoking in Leviticus 18 and 20 the sexual relations between two men within the context of incestuous relations, the Bible establishes an analogy between the two, undoubtedly because it fears a similar danger in the two cases: the danger of a confusion of roles that threatens the harmony of familial relations. According to this exegesis, which is based on the context in which we find two prohibitions against homosexual relations, the reason that explains this prohibition is familial or social. The latter would be in danger if homosexual relations were possible in a way that is analogous to sexual relations between close relatives. We must therefore deepen this analogy which the context of Leviticus 18 and 20 seems to establish between the two prohibitions.[5]

What is common to the three explanations of the prohibition of homosexual relations in Leviticus 18 and 20 is that all three reasons are social, not personal. They see the religious and cultural identity of the people of Israel, or the fecundity and the numerous offspring that it is supposed to protect, or familial harmony that could be harmed by the carnal desires of one of its members for another. Quite unlike today, it seems that the Bible's concern is not that of the desire of happiness

---

5. Because of the considerable importance and influence of the monumental and erudite commentary that Jacob Milgrom wrote on the book of Leviticus, allow me to base my explanations of the prohibition of homosexual relations in Leviticus 18 and 20 in dialogue with him: (1) The common trait of the lists of prohibitions in Leviticus 18 and 20 is procreation, p. 1567. But this cannot be possible since a number of incestuous relations are fecund. (2) In response, Milgrom says that in these cases procreation is illicit. But whence comes its illicit nature? The reason for this cannot be procreation since it can be fecund. If we wish to avoid a circular argument, we have to find another common denominator that is either licit or illicit procreation. (3) Milgrom is surprised at not finding a prohibition against masturbation, p. 1567f. If it were a question of forbidding semen to be wasted it should have been mentioned. Milgrom explains this silence because Leviticus 18 and 20 is considering only sexual relations, not solely the loss of semen. Now, in addition to procreation, sexual relations imply a social dimension, that is, either liceity or illiceity. These do not depend on the fecundity or the sterility of these relations, but on their place in the social system or their exclusion from it. In Genesis 19 and Judges 19, the offense against hospitality is made concrete in the carnal desires of the men with respect to one who is a foreigner and therefore less protected than a native of the region. Innocent Himbaza shows this in his contribution to this book. Why did the narrators choose this form of sin to illustrate their lack of hospitality? The sin of the people of Sodom and of Gibeah consisted in the violence of the strong (the men of Sodom and Gibeah) against the weaker family (that of Lot and that of the Ephraimite), for while they were being shown hospitality, the host is a privileged member of the family that receives them. Thus the evil committed is the destruction of the protected familial order. Clearly, this has nothing to do with procreation.

of the individual who is attracted to someone else. This difference, between a perspective that is especially concerned with community or social interests and a perspective that is more focused on individual needs, can be quite profound.

In a general sense, we can affirm that the Bible does not conceive of complete personal happiness outside of a human community. Community is an indispensable condition of individual happiness. Gen. 2:18 expresses this conviction in this way: "It is not good for the man to be alone." One cannot be happy alone. Full happiness includes belonging to a happy community. Even the Song of Songs, which celebrates the joy of two lovers in their mutual love, seems to suggest this indispensable horizon of the larger community for the love between two persons, since chapter 6, verse 9 talks about the mother's love for her daughter, the beloved one of the Song of Songs. The mother's love for her daughter is like a needed nest to house the love of the two lovers. In the Bible, individual and communal happiness are perhaps less far apart from each other than we would expect from a modern perspective.

The Benefit of Clear Familial Relations

The human experience that is expressed in Leviticus 18 is for the need of limits to sexual desire. Left to itself, sexual desire would run the risk of wreaking havoc on communities. Peace and humanity cannot reign there except when rules protecting certain relationships from disordered desires, for example, adults with respect to children, are recognized.[6] Two verses in Leviticus 18, vv. 17–18, which correspond to Lev. 20:14 and 17, suggest this reason as the motive that in-

6. Or again of a population with respect to guests, as seen in Genesis 19 and Judges 19. Cf. Innocent Himbaza's contribution to this volume.

spired all of the commandments contained in Leviticus 18 and 20 and, among which, is found the prohibition of sexual relations between men: Lev. 18:22 and 20:13. Lev. 18:17–18 and 20:14, 17 directly concern two prohibitions against polygamy. According to them, the same man cannot marry a mother and her daughter or two sisters.[7] Why? It is easy to understand. Two wives of the same husband inevitably find themselves rivals. For a husband cannot love both of them with the same love, even if he is a good husband—recall, for example, the husband of Hannah and Peninah in 1 Samuel 1. As a consequence, the two women will see themselves in a situation of inequality, one always fearing that she is less dear to her husband than the other wife or that she will lose her preferred status. Thus marriage will force them into a contest because of the very conditions of their marriage.

Now this is even more cruel and inhuman when it comes to two women joined together by a deep mutual affection as is the case of a mother and her daughter (recall here Song of Songs 6:9) or two sisters. The source of their natural and strong affection is their familial relationship. The daughter is the fruit of her mother's body. It was she who gave birth to her, and she was her first educator, who helped her prepare for life. Two sisters are like two brothers of which Scripture says that a "brother is born for the times of adversity" (Prov. 17:17). This means that brothers and sisters are the

7. A. Tosato, *Il matrimonia. Una teoria generale*, Analecta biblica 100 (Rome: Biblical Institute Press, 1982), 209, suggests that the term "two sisters" means two Israelite women and that this would be place where the Israelite Law promulgated monogamous marriage. This thesis is ingenious and seductive. But the entire context of Leviticus 18 and 20 takes the expressions dealing with familial relationship in the narrow sense of the relative positions of persons within the family structure. This is why it is probable that the term "sisters" means women born from the same parents and not merely fellow countrymen.

most solid source of help that life has given them. For brothers and sisters are closer to each other than any other person, especially once the parents die. Toward whom should one turn for help in times of need or danger, in a hostile and indifferent world, if not toward one's own brother or sister? Brothers and sisters know that they belong to each other. Certainly the Bible does not tire of reminding us over and over again of crises in fraternal relations: between Cain and Abel (Genesis 4), Jacob and Esau (Genesis 27), Joseph and his brothers (Genesis 37), among the sons of David (2 Samuel 13–15 and 1 Kings 1). But these crises reveal precisely the abyss of evil that occurs when brothers become enemies. A brother who is an enemy is infinitely worse than a non-fraternal enemy, because his real role as brother should have been to safeguard the lives of his brothers and sisters.

The biblical thought expressed in these two family laws gives primacy of place to familial relations that go back to birth. These relations are givens that mark the whole of our lives from the outset. They irreversibly bind parents and children, brothers and sisters. They are human capital until the day we die. One should not hide this treasure by burying it under other future human relationships (such as marriage) that come into existence not by birth but by sexual desire. This desire must defer to familial relations. Where it does not, for example, when a son of David, Amnon, rapes his sister Tamar out of lust (cf. 2 Samuel 13), relations become inhuman and violence and violation erupt within the very heart of the family.

It thus becomes possible to understand the prohibition against incest in general found in Leviticus 18 and 20. This prohibition is at the service of making clear relations that are created by family and by marriage. Both types of relations are precious for the lives of individuals. They must be preserved and protected. There should be no contest between the two, for this would lead to both social and psychological confusion. One would not know what role to play: that of the mother attached to her daughter, or that of the jealous wife of the second spouse who also happens to be one's daughter; or again, that of the sister who knows she is responsible for her sister and wants to be of service to her in her need, or that of the married woman suspicious of the other wife who is her own sister. Everyone benefits from clear relations between members of a family, both the entire family unit itself as well as each member of that family. Familial relations bring with them both affection and a sense of belonging. As for relations that are born out of the attraction that persons have for each other, they enrich the family by gifts of love and ensure descendants for generations to come.[8]

The Prohibition of Homosexual Relations within the Context of Incest Taboos

Since the two passages in the Law of Moses that forbid homosexual relations are either close to the prohibitions against incest (Lev. 18:22), or integrated within a list of such prohibitions (Lev. 20:13), the two prohibitions seem, in the eyes of the authors of these two chapters, to have something in common. These authors wish to safeguard the roles of each member of the family in their specificity. A close relative

8. This exegesis of Leviticus 18 and 20 was already proposed (with many more details) in the eighteenth century by one of the greatest exegetes of the time, known for his work on the Mosaic Law: J. D. Michaelis, *Abhandlung von den Ehegesetzen Mosis welche die Heyrathen in die nahe Freundschaft ungtersagen*, 2. und vermehrte Aufl. Göttingen: Abraham Vanderhoeck's seel (Witwe, 1768).

must play the role of father, mother, son, daughter, brother or sister; but the role must not be that of the lover of one's parents, one's children, or one's siblings. In a family that has not only parents but servants as well as domestic animals living all together, relations are multiple and complex. They risk at each moment becoming even more complicated. This is why anything that can simplify these relations is welcome. The attraction between members of the opposite sex is difficult enough without adding to it the complication of love between two men. For the love relations between men add to occasions of friction within the family. Should one distinguish between licit and illicit affective relations between men in the same way that one distinguishes licit and illicit relations between members of the opposite sex who are closely related by a series of additional prohibitions against incest? The Law of Moses chose a much simpler and radical solution in forbidding all sexual relations between men. Perhaps this option was chosen because of the sterility of homosexual love, which is incapable of providing descendants.

If this explanation of the prohibitions found in Lev. 18:22 and 20:13 in its proper context is correct, we can draw the following conclusions from our previous analysis: sexual attraction between men and women needs to be guided by rules in order to avoid dehumanization and violence in family relations. In order to avoid additional complication by allowing sexual relations between men (and one could add, between women), which would introduce additional tensions in a family group, the Law of Moses had recourse to a complete exclusion of such relations, more so because they do not provide descendants.

We must repeat: the point of view would be that of the family group and its need to be transparent in its relations between members. The search for happiness of individual persons through their affective desires is not taken into consideration, in contrast with what is the first concern today. Moreover, one can ask the question: Were the conditions of the Israelite family life back then so different from conditions in the modern West that the same rules might not be applied to both? In order to answer this essential question, we must first resituate the prohibitions found in Lev. 18:22 and 20:13 in their proper historical and literary contexts.

The Literary Context of Leviticus 18:22 and 20:13

The Literary Context of Lev. 18:6–18

It makes more sense to analyze Leviticus 18 first, and on its own merits before turning to Leviticus 20. Then, we will look at both of them together within the context of the Book of Leviticus.[9]

After the prologue (Lev. 18:1–5), mentioned previously, the chapter is made up of a list of fifteen prohibitions concerning family relations (Lev. 18:6–18), followed by a further five prohibitions (Lev. 18:19–23) that deal not with incest but with other prohibited acts, among which are homosexual relations between men (Lev. 18:23). The chapter ends with a long exhortation (Lev. 18:24–30).

The heart of Leviticus 18 is a listing of the fourteen relationships deemed to be incestuous (Lev. 18:7–18). These are prefaced by a general rule:

LEVITICUS 18:6 (RSV): [6] "None of you shall approach any one near of kin to him to uncover nakedness. I am the LORD."

9. For details, cf. Milgrom, *Leviticus 17–22* and A. Schenker, "Incest Prohibitions" for explanatory notes.

The expression "to uncover nakedness" is a metonymic way of referring to sexual intercourse. The aim of these fourteen specific prohibitions stands out with great clarity in Lev. 18:17–18. As we have seen, they guarantee humanity and peace to the family unit. They do so by freeing family relations, founded on birth and marriage, from the grip of desires that could emerge later and obscure the transparency of existing familial relations.

The Literary Context of Lev. 18:19–23

In all likelihood the five following prohibitions (vv. 19–23) had been attached to the fifteen previous ones because of close connection to them, even though their immediate purpose is not the protection of familial relations. Verse 19 forbids sexual relations with a woman during menstruation; verse 20 proscribes adultery; verse 21, situated in the middle of the five prohibitions, prohibits the burnt-offering of a child to Molech; verse 22 excludes sexual relations between two men; verse 23 proscribes sexual relations with an animal. These prohibitions are less unified than those of verses 7–18, which deal with any marriage whatsoever, whether it be monogamous or polygamous (vv. 7–16), or polygamy specifically (vv. 17–18). But each one of these five prohibitions also directly concerns the family. Not to have sexual relations with one's wife during her period implies that, even within the family, a limit is imposed on the sexual desires of the husband, regardless of the motive. Sexual desire is not an absolute need. It must take the back seat to other needs in certain circumstances. Adultery is proscribed in order to protect the wife (or wives) living within the family, and thus the family itself, from outside aggression.

A child must not be burned for Molech, not only because

this is an act of idolatry and a particularly cruel type of murder, but because a healthy child is a blessing given to the family by the Lord. To destroy a blessing, which is always a gift of life, is a serious evil. A proverb, cited by God himself in Es. 65:8, says it in a particularly striking way. The juice that swells each grape of the vine matured without the work of man. It sprouted during the summer. In the fall it is still there, increasing in value, a fruit, a delicious gain that one can taste and that quenches the thirst and that nature—or God!—places there. It represents, or better yet is, a blessing. How much truer is it of the fruit of the womb. It is a blessing given by the Creator (cf. Gen. 1:28). The family exists for this blessing. Moreover, children should be able to live within the bosom of the family protected from all danger of aggression against them. They have the right to enjoy the security that their parents and siblings must provide them.

As for bestiality, it is contrary to the distinction between humans and animals (who often live in close proximity to one another ([cf. 2 Sam. 12:3]) and, as a consequence, opposed to the dignity of human sexuality. Moreover, it excludes the possibility of procreation.[10]

Lev. 18:22 *in Particular*

In the collection of five prohibitions, homosexual relations, mentioned in verse 22, are placed in symmetry with adultery. In the center of this concentrically arranged list is thus

10. Milgrom, *Leviticus* 17–22, p. 1530, lists both the ancient and the modern exegetes who explain the common denominator of Leviticus 18 (and 20) as I have done here. Ibn Kaspi, Samuel David Luzzatto, Karl Elliger, and others deny this explanation because of the five prohibitions in Lev. 18:19–23. But it seems like these five commandments are part of the global intention to ensure the security of each family member and to protect the family unit against sexual excess and, in the case of verse 21, idolatry.

found the sacrifice of children to Moloch. This act is the most abominable. This center is framed immediately by the prohibition of adultery in verse 20 and that of homosexual relations between two men in verse 22; at the edge of this circle is the sexual relations of a husband with his menstruating wife in verse 19, on the one hand, and, on the other hand, sexual relations with an animal in verse 23. This symmetrical position suggests an analogous fear regarding both acts. Both jeopardize the safety of the family: one from inside, the other from the outside. In fact, the sexual relation between men superimposes itself on the parental role that they must exercise and on the social position that they occupy within the family structure. For some are chiefs, the others are servants. Some must obey, others exercise power. Some are young, others are old. If to this one adds the role of lover and beloved in the erotic sense of the term, the roles are in danger of falling into confusion. The difference of these various roles exercised simultaneously would create added tensions in a setting where centrifugal forces are already numerous. The stories of the families of Isaac, Jacob, Laban, and the sons of Jacob (Gen. 27–33:37), or of the house of David allow us to glimpse the potential for anarchy that arises from pitting the men of the same family group against one another. Moreover, the stories of these conflicts reveal that families are ill-equipped to handle conflicts among the males of the family. Deuteronomy 21:18–21 gives another example.

The Audience of Leviticus 18

We should conclude the overall analysis of Leviticus 18 with a remark about its form and the audience to whom its prohibitions are addressed. The prohibitions are directed to a married Israelite male whom the Lord addresses with the second person singular: you. The relations of family and of marriage, whether licit or illicit, and acts that are prohibited or permitted, are specifically addressed to him. This is why in Lev. 18:22 only the sexual relations between two men are considered. But the commandments and the laws of the Old Testament also have an analogical weight for similar or comparable cases to those that are specifically mentioned. So for example, the lists of goods to be coveted in the Decalogue—house, wife, animals, fields, and servants—is not exhaustive (cf. Ex. 20:17; Dt. 5:21). It is also forbidden to covet a vine, even though it is not mentioned here. But the story of Naboth's vineyard in 1 Kings 20 shows the grave fault committed by King Ahab in coveting that vine. Consequently, what the Lord forbids explicitly to the head of the Israelite family in Leviticus 18 (and 20) is implicitly and proportionally forbidden to all other Israelites, both men and women. Homosexual relations between men, which are specified in Lev. 18:22 directly, implicitly concern those of women. This was already Paul's interpretation in Rom. 1:26, where the prohibition is extended to women.

The Literary Context of Leviticus 20

Leviticus 20 has as its centerpiece a list of twelve prohibited unions or sexual acts (Lev. 20:10–21), and among them is found homosexual relations between men (v. 13). One can immediately see that this list has four unique characteristics. First, the offense is stated, not in the second person by the direct address "you" as in Leviticus 18, but in a conditional or casuistic phrase: "if someone." Second, all of the faults listed are committed by two people. To be realized, they have need of two people who want to commit them or who, at least, consent to them.

Third, all of them are subject to the death penalty except for Lev. 20:21. It is probable that capital punishment, the worst that there is, can be explained by the fact that two people are involved, both of whom agree to commit it. Mutual consent adds an aggravating circumstance to a forbidden act, because the threshold of personal shame before others has been crossed in order to recruit an accomplice needed to commit the act. Thus the fault is doubled: the evil act itself and the seduction leading to the corruption of someone in order to bring about the evil. Adam and Eve illustrate this type of fault committed together (Genesis 3), and even more importantly, Ahab, who consented to the crimes perpetrated by his wife against Naboth (cf. 1 Kings 20). This is why Paul can qualify consent or approval as more serious than the sin itself (Rom 1.32). This analysis of a fault committed by two people together explains the severity of the penalty pronounced against someone who has sexual relations with a menstruating woman as well as against the woman herself (v. 18), while involuntary sexual contact, that is, sexual contact with a woman whom one did not know was having her period, brings with it only a light impurity with no sanctions (cf. Lev. 15:24). In fact, Leviticus 20 deals only with cases that are intentional or premeditated. In the first instance, one person supports another person in his or her intention to commit evil secretly rather than resisting it (cf. Dt. 13:7–12). The story of Joseph in Egypt, for example, recounts an attempt to seduce someone for a hidden evil act that could not be done without the other's complicity (cf. Gen. 39:7–12). The same notion stands behind the idea of inflicting the death penalty on two men having sexual relations with each other (v. 13).

Why the Death Penalty (Leviticus 20:13)?

The Death Penalty Is Used as a Warning, Not as a Penal Norm

It is rather certain that the death penalty imposed on the two partners of a homosexual relation is *the most shocking* of all that the Bible says on homosexuality. This penalty is intolerable for modern sensibilities. Whatever our reservations may be concerning this type of sexuality, that one should kill those who practice it seems rightly barbarous and inhuman. Now, it is precisely because a first reading of the texts is unacceptable that we have a particular need to read and interpret them with care in their context. Unless we do so, we risk succumbing to a false interpretation of the text and making it say what it does not say.

Thus let us look at the fourth characteristic of the faults listed in Leviticus 20. We notice that the twelve incestuous acts of Leviticus 20, with the sole exception of Lev. 20:19, will all be punished with death, but the Lord himself will put to death spouses who have sexual relations during the wife's period (Lev. 20:18).[11] The death penalty is not only the result of punitive human justice. Moreover, the severity is not restricted to the homosexual act as such; it does not single out this act but, more generally, is imposed on illicit sexual acts performed in secret. In point of fact, in all of these

11. According to Lev. 15:24 the man who sleeps with his wife during her period incurs only a slight impurity, which creates a week of impurity after which he is pure. How does one explain the apparent contradiction between Lev. 15:19, 24 (impurity for a day for the woman and a week for the man) and Lev. 20:18 (the death penalty for both of them)? The simplest explanation begins with the observation that in Lev. 20, all forbidden sexual relations are expressly willed, while the bodily fluids of Lev. 15:19-32 occur spontaneously and therefore involuntarily. Consequently, Lev. 15:24 considers an unforeseen menstruation, coming unexpectedly during or after sexual relations, while Lev. 20:18 focuses on deliberate sexual intercourse in spite of the woman's period.

cases envisioned in Leviticus 20, the two persons involved in the particular act in question consent to it in secret. Normally, they are the only ones who are witnesses to what they do. It can easily be seen that when a hidden transgression is committed without anyone knowing about it, there will be no setting right, because of a lack of charges! It will necessarily remain unpunished and it can be charged therefore, according to an ancient perspective, to the entire community.[12] This community would in fact be dangerously charged with a disorder that remained secret and therefore without reparation. Deuteronomy 21:1–9 described a crime, a murder, whose perpetrator remains unknown, and the measures that the community must take to avert the consequences of that crime falling upon them. It is therefore in the interest of the entire community, and of the persons at fault themselves, that the damage be eliminated by compensatory acts. Now, it is precisely the great severity of the sanctions that will cause fear in the hearts of the guilty, who will not be able to trivialize their act; out of fear, they will of their own accord confess their fault to the priests and by doing so transform the severe penalty into something lighter, as can be seen in Lev. 5:5, 20–26. Two further stories, Joshua 7 and 1 Sam. 14:36–45, show the curse of a hidden fault on the entire community and the community's effort to uncover it. 1 Samuel describes in particular how the death penalty, already decreed, can be commuted right after the discovery of the guilty one into an act of grace in his favor (1 Sam. 14:45).[13]

12. The fear of groups in ancient times to suffer the consequences of faults committed in secret and therefore not reconciled is particularly highlighted by J. Milgrom, *Cult and Conscience: The Asham and the Priestly Doctrine of Repentance*. Studies in Judaism in Late Antiquity 18 (Leiden: Brill, 1976), 74–83 and passim (Milgrom does not speak about Lev. 20).

13. T. Hieke, "Das Alte Testament und die Todesstrafe," *Biblica* 85 (2004): 349–74.

In summary, if the penalty is so severe it is ultimately to move those responsible for the fault committed in secret to foresee its terrible consequences and freely admit to it and offer to make reparation. This seems to me the only way to reconcile the apparent contradiction in Leviticus 20 between faults that would normally remain hidden and their extremely severe sanction, and to explain that, in the case of sexual relations with a woman during her period, it is not the human court, but God's, which is competent to impose a penalty. The severe penalty that threatens secret evil-doers disturbs their consciences to the point that they will prefer to free themselves from its weight by confessing the fault and settling accounts in place of a penalty mandated by the Law. These penalties are not *executed* but rather *commuted* in an act of grace and by compensation. This is beneficial both for the guilty and for the entire community, itself freed from a fault that had not been rectified.

The Structure of Leviticus 20

Each of the twelve sexually illicit acts of Lev. 20:10–21 corresponds to a symmetric prohibition, already discussed, in Leviticus 18. The list found in Leviticus 20 is made up of three parts. The first, verses 10–12, proscribe three acts committed by an Israelite that wounds other families. The second, verses 13–16, lists four sexual unions that can be committed within the family itself by a fellow family member. In this section, in verse 13, the sexual relations between two men are prohibited. This prohibition is immediately followed in verse 14 by one that forbids a husband in a polygamous marriage to marry at the same time both a mother and her daughter (cf. Lev. 18:17). The placing together of these two prohibitions suggests perhaps that the two love relations in the eyes of the legislator are somehow connected, their common characteristic being the confusion of roles that must remain distinct for fear of compromising familial unity and peace. The third section, verses 17–21, excludes five illicit relations with women who are related by blood or marriage, and also with a woman who is menstruating.

In sum, the central list of Lev. 20:10–21 does not separate incestuous relations from other illicit sexual unions. They are aligned without distinction. Thus it is suggested that they are not really distinct. Perhaps the reason for this notion resides in the power of sexual attraction to introduce anarchy and rivalry into the family, thereby dehumanizing relations among persons. Sexuality is dangerous when it gives free rein to sexual impulses in a disorderly fashion.

In addition to the central list, Leviticus 20 also condemns parents who sacrifice their children to Moloch to be burned alive (vv. 2–6), children who curse their parents (v. 9) and the practice of divinization (vv. 6 and 27). The chapter ends with a conclusion (vv. 22–24) that is connected to the conclusion found in Lev. 18:24–30.

Summary Conclusion of Leviticus 18–20

The two conclusions of Leviticus 18 and 20 make of these three chapters a unified whole. In fact, in all of the Bible, the metaphorical expression of the earth vomiting up its inhabitants occurs only in the conclusions of these two chapters, at Lev. 18:25, 28, and 20:22. Now, the country was about to vomit up its inhabitants the first time before the entrance the Israelites leaving Egypt, but it could again vomit up the Israelites if they conducted themselves in the way of the previous inhabitants. How did they in fact behave? Precisely by not observing the prohibitions of Leviticus 18 and 20 as well as those found in Leviticus 19, a chapter that is sandwiched in between the symmetrical conclusions of Lev. 18:24–30 and Lev. 20:22–24. These three chapters outline the conditions necessary to remain in the country. If the Israelites obey these laws and rules, the country will not vomit them out. These two conclusions highlight the importance of the commandments found in Leviticus 18–20. Even though these commandments are not part of the revealed laws of Mount Sinai, the continued existence of the Israelites in their country depends on their being followed. Leviticus 18 and 19 are joined together by the use of the following formula: "I am the Lord your God" (Lev. 18:2, 4, 30; 19:3, 4, 10, 25, 31, 34, 36), or "I am the Lord" (Lev. 18:5, 6, 21; 19:12, 14, 18, 28, 30, 32, 37). The meaning of the formula is to express the necessary authority to oblige or authorize an inferior person, as it is found in the more profane use of this formula in Gen. 41:44.[14] Furthermore, Leviticus 19 and 20 are joined together by the theme of the holiness of the Lord: 19:2; 20:7–8, 26. Thus the unity of the whole of these three chapters is reinforced.

These three chapters form their own section of the Holiness Code (Leviticus 17–26). According to the redactional conclusion of Lev. 18:24–30, the keeping of the laws of Lev. 18:6–23 will make the inhabitants pure (vv. 24 and 30) and the country as well (vv. 25 and 28). The neglect of these rules will sully the land. There is only one other biblical passage that calls the Promised Land sullied by the inhabitants who preceded the Israelites, and this is Ezra 9:11–12.

14. A. Schenker, "Der Monotheismus in erster Gebot, die Stellung der Frau in Sabbatgebot und zwei andere Sachfragen zum Dekalog" in A. Schenker, *Text und Sinn im Alten Testament. Text geschichtliche und bibeltheologishche Studien.* Orbis Biblicus et Orientalis 103 (Göttingen: Vandenhoeck & Ruprecht, 1991), 188–92.

There Ezra saw the absolute necessity of dissolving mixed marriages, in which a number of Judeans lived. For, in these marriages, one could not clearly distinguish blood and married relations within the family, since these other peoples ignored these laws and did not conduct themselves as the Israelites did, whereas it is precisely the Israelites' observance that constituted the indispensable condition for perduring in the land![15]

The Historical Context of Leviticus 18 and 20

The conclusions of Lev. 18:24–30 and 20:22–24 belong to a period close to the time of Ezra (as does the book known by his name), since they express the same understanding of what is required for Israel to keep possession of the land and not lose it, as the former inhabitants had. Nevertheless, the substance of the rules ordering licit and illicit sexual relations within families do not date from the time of Ezra, in the fifth or at the beginning of the fourth centuries B.C. Such rules are deeply rooted in minds and consciences. This is why they change rarely and not easily. The preceding analysis suggests an origin within a social situation in which families form the principal community to which individuals belong, while other social structures, such as the kingdom or the state or the communal organization of a city, exercise a lesser influence over the lives of individuals.

In sum, more here than elsewhere perhaps, it is neces-

15. A. Schenker, "Propheten schon vor Mose und Esra, Verbot der Mischehen: zwei ungelöste Probleme im Esrabuch" in *Studien su Propheten und Religionsgeschichte*, ed. A. Schenker Stuttgarter biblische Aufsatzbände. A.T. 36 (Stuttgart: Katholik Bibelwerk, 2003) 132–39.

sary to distinguish the time of the composition of the text of Leviticus 18 and 20 from the time of the origins of the rules governing families, marriages, and licit and illicit sexual acts. These may be much earlier.

This chronology is confirmed by the perspective we find in Lev. 18:24–30 and 20:22–24. For the country that vomits out its inhabitants when they no longer observe the rules of life found in Leviticus 18–20 is an allusion to the Babylonian Captivity where Judah (Israel) is taken off into exile after losing the land. Its perspective is comparable to that found in Dt. 4:27–31, 30:1–10, and 1 Kgs. 8:46–50. These passages can be dated to decades following the exile.

The Significance of Leviticus 18:22 and 20:13 from the Perspective of Biblical Theology

The analysis of the two prohibitions against homosexual relations between men, both from their proper context and in light of the conclusions of these two chapters (Lev. 18:24–30; 20:22–24), shows first of all the importance that attaches to them. These are not ritual commandments of minor significance.

Second, as we have already said, these two passages are less concerned with the individual's pursuit of happiness than with the good of the family. They express the belief that homosexual relations would harm the cohesion of a human community already exposed, without them, to a number of fracturing pressures. In view of the precarious nature of this community, which is vital for the subsistence of individuals, risks should not be taken to plant further seeds of anarchy, as would happen if the male members had sexual relations among themselves in addition to those existing between men and women. These latter, because of new births, are in any case, indispensable in order to assure the future of the family and its older members.

It is also clear, and this is the third point, that the prohibition is against sexual relations between men, not against their inclinations. Logically speaking, it must be added that anything that paves the way for the prohibited act is also excluded by the Torah.

Fourth, it is important to recall that the Law speaks directly of sexual relations between men. But in virtue of the force of analogy possessed by ethical or moral commandments and biblical rules for proper living, these same laws can be applied equally to comparable situations not specifically addressed by the commandments of the rule. A law is always capable of a number of applications that are implied in its formulation. This becomes clear in the light of new situations that are interpreted analogously with those envisaged by the text. This is why we can state the probability that, according to the Bible, sexual relations between women is also prohibited. This is how the apostle Paul interpreted Lev. 18:22 and 20:13.

Fifth, biblical theology, understood here as theology explicitly or implicitly contained in the Bible, often leads to a critical question posed to contemporary human thought. In the case of homosexual behavior, and in light of the analysis of Lev. 18:20, the question that the Bible can raise with respect to contemporary thought is this: does not homosexuality that is lived and publicly recognized contribute to the disintegration of a society already prey to disintegration? Does not Lev. 18:20 also suggest a conception which sees sexuality from a perspective that is both personal and communal? These questions should be studied more deeply in dialogue with several disciplines that go beyond the scope of the exegetical study.

The sixth point creates a bridge between the Torah of the Old Testament and the apostle Paul. As a Pharisee and one who is knowledgeable in the Torah, Paul could not ignore the weight of Leviticus 18 and 20. Taking up this teaching for Christians living in Rome, he moves beyond Leviticus to creation, as Jean-Baptiste Edart shows elsewhere in this volume. In point of fact, Paul must have developed a theological framework that takes into account this commandment. He did this by having recourse to creation and the Lord's blessing to men.

3 The New Testament and Homosexuality

It is only reasonable that, in examining the Bible regarding homosexuality, we look also at the New Testament, which Christians understand as the fulfillment and key of divine revelation. The texts explicitly discussing this question are very few in number and are found exclusively in the Pauline corpus. This is why studies have essentially focused on Rom. 1:18–32 on the one hand, and on 1 Cor. 6:9 and 1 Tim. 1:10 on the other hand. The first text offers a long development on the consequences of idolatry on the moral life. The other two are lists of vices that include two terms that can refer to homosexual practices: *malakos* and *arsenokoitēs*. This is why we begin our study with these texts.

The gospels have nothing explicit to say about homosexuality. This silence, connected to the great mercy of Jesus with respect to sinners, is sometimes interpreted as indicating that Jesus implicitly approves of homosexuality. Recent studies also see this in certain texts: the healing of the slave of the Roman centurion (Mt. 8:6–13; Lk. 7:1–10) and the figure of the Beloved Disciple. It seems helpful to us to consider the evidence we have that witnesses to Jesus' attitude regarding human sexuality, in order to test the interpretation of his silence on homosexuality. We will also examine the texts used to see if, in fact, they justify this reading. Finally, a number of preachers consider that it is contrary to the commandment of love of neighbor to offer a negative judgment on homosexuality. We will conclude our study with the meaning of this commandment and its implications for homosexual persons.

Paul of Tarsus

1 *Corinthians* 6:9–10 *and* 1 *Timothy* 1:10

1 CORINTHIANS 6:9–10 (NAB): [9] Do you not know that the unjust will not inherit the kingdom of God? Do not be deceived; neither fornicators nor idolaters nor adulterers nor boy prostitutes (*malakoi*) nor practicing homosexuals (*arsenokoitai*) [10] nor thieves nor the greedy nor drunkards nor slanderers nor robbers will inherit the kingdom of God.

The diversity of opinions on how best to translate *malakos* and *arsenokoitēs* shows the difficulty of the question and the unease of translators![1] The difficulty is due to the uncommonness and the originality of these terms which appear only in the Pauline letters. *Arsenokoitēs* appears here for the first time in all of Greek literature. The unease stems from the harshness of the judgment laid upon them: persons designated by these terms will not inherit the kingdom of God. Because of this, any translation in the current debate on the question of homosexuality takes on an added weight.

The Pauline letters contain a number of lists of vices. These lists were frequently found in the literature of the first century and their catalogue-like structures helped in memorization. In the case of Paul, these lists are simple repetitions used to illustrate an idea more easily. The lists written by the apostle are often detailed, which can be seen clearly

1. Note that the second edition of the New American Bible (NAB) does not hesitate to call them "practicing homosexuals" in certain cases.

here: five of the ten vices are sexual, recalling the situation described in 1 Corinthians 5–6; the other five call to mind the difficulties found in 1 Corinthians 11.[2] This list concludes a section begun in 1 Corinthians 5.1. Paul reproves the Corinthian community for a double scandal: it tolerates an incestuous relationship in its midst and it dares to have recourse to pagan tribunals to settle lawsuits between its members. The Christians had been "washed, sanctified, justified," while the pagans will not inherit the kingdom of heaven. To tolerate incest is to allow the presence of a most serious sin in the midst of a holy people; like the yeast that makes the dough rise, this runs the risk of corrupting the entire community, the people of the New Covenant invited to celebrate Easter (1 Cor. 5:7–8). In the same way, to have recourse to a pagan tribunal leaves the Corinthians unable to maintain their identity and integrity as a holy people of God when, as in Israel, there had existed a long tradition of exercising justice among the people (Ex. 18:21–27).

In 1 Corinthians 6:9 Paul repeats the same list as in 5:11 adding to it four terms: "adulterers," "*malakoi,*" "*arsenokoitai,*" and "thieves." This list refers directly back to 1 Corinthians 5. In fact, outside of the added terms which, with the exception of "thieves," have a sexual connotation, let us note the position of "fornicators" (*pornoi*) at the head of the list, the same word used to designate the incestuous man in 5:1. This construction also prepares the groundwork for the development following verses 6:12–20, whose principle theme is sexual license. It is in this context that our two words must be interpreted. This is confirmed by the words

2. For additional information of this precise point, see K. Bailey, "Paul's Theological Foundation for Human Sexuality: 1 Cor 6:12–20 in the Light of Rhetorical Criticism," *Near East School of Theology Theological Review* 3 (1980): 27–41.

that immediately precede *malakoi* and *arsenokoitai*, name-ly, adulterers (*moichoi*) and fornicators (*pornoi*).

Passive and Active

Malakos literally means "soft, silky, delicate."[3] In a homo-sexual relation, it designates the passive partner.[4] It has a very negative connotation. The difficulty with this term tak-en by itself is that it can refer to different realities: a male prostitute, a transvestite, an effeminate man, etc. It can therefore be understood either in a very narrow sense (male prostitute) or in a wider one (an effeminate man who takes excessive care of his appearance), making it difficult to identify the referent.

The literary context can help us. Here we are dealing with sexual matters, thereby excluding the wider meaning of the term. We are talking about sexual behavior. But in or-der to understand the precise meaning of the term, we must have recourse to extrabiblical sources.

Philo of Alexandria uses *malakia* to designate the behav-ior of passive homosexual partners concerned about their effeminate appearance in order to please their masculine lover.[5] In the same way, in his description of the men of So-dom, Philo uses the term *malakotēs* to characterize the atti-tude of penetrated males.[6] These two recurrences show that

3. See Lk. 7:25 and Mt. 11:8, where the adjective is used to qualify cloth-ing and can be translated as "delicate."

4. In his translation of *Tardarum Passionum Libri* (a work on chron-ic illnesses) of Soranos of Ephesus, Caelius Aurelianus, a doctor during the reigns of Trajan and Adrian, titles the part on men who desire to be pen-etrated: "Concerning the soft ones or *subacti* who are called by the Greeks *malthakoi*" (4.9.131–37).

5. *De Specialibus Legibus* III and IV. Introduction, Translation and Notes by A. Mosès in *Oeuvres de Philon d'Alexandrie* 25 (Paris: Editions du Cerf, 1970) 3:37–42 (particularly 3.39–40).

6. *De Abrahamo*. Introduction, Translation and Notes by J. Gorez in *Oeuvres de Philon d'Alexandrie* 20 (Paris: Editions du Cerf, 1966) 135–37.

malakos designates not only male prostitutes but any passive partner in a male homosexual relation. In our estimation, it is impossible to define more precisely the nature of these *malakoi* at this point in our study.

An analysis of *arsenokoitēs* reveals no ambiguity. This term literally means "sleeping (*koitē*: lit. "bed, couch," *keisthai*: "to be asleep") with a man (*arsen*: "male")." Formed by the association of two words present in Lv. 18:22 and 20:13, it very probably appeared in a Judeo-Hellenistic context. The Greek text of Lev. 18:22 says: "With a man (*arsenos*) you will not sleep (*koimēthēsē*) as one sleeps (*koitēn*) with a woman. It is an abomination." Lev. 20:13 is even more explicit: "Whoever sleeps (*koimēthē*) with a man (*aresenos*) [as] one sleeps (*koitēn*) with a woman, it is an abomination that the two have committed, they must die, their blood will be on them." In the Greek text, "man" (*arsenos*) and "slept" (*koitēn*) follow one another, facilitating the formation of a neologism. This construction finds an echo in the rabbinic tradition. The rabbis used the Hebrew expression "to sleep with a male" (*miškab zâkûr*) taken from the Hebrew text of Lev. 18:22 and Lev. 20:13 to talk about homosexual relations.[7] They do not limit this to pederasty. All of these elements seem sufficient to affirm that in 1 Cor. 6:9 the term refers explicitly to men having an active role in homosexual relations. The postbiblical usage of this term confirms this meaning.[8] The Latin translation of the Vulgate,[9] *masculorum concubitores* (a man sleeping with males), express-

7. See Talmud of Babylon, *Sanhedrin* 54a; Talmud of Babylon, *Shabbat* 17b; Talmud of Babylon, *Sukkah* 29a; Talmud of Jerusalem, *Berakot* 9.50.13c.

8. For a presentation of the principle recurrences, see R. A. J. Gagnon, *The Bible and Homosexual Practice: Texts and Hermeneutics* (Nashville, TN: Abingdon Press, 2001), 317–22.

9. Translation done by Saint Jerome in the fourth century. It became *the* Bible of the entire Latin tradition.

es clearly the fact that the term did not suffer from ambiguity in the fourth century.

Now that we have clarified the meaning of *arsenokoitēs*, we can give a more precise definition of *malakos* in 1 Cor. 6:9. In effect, we have in this verse two complimentary terms. The first makes explicit reference to an active behavior in a homosexual relation. The second very frequently refers to the passive role. The presence of the first term allows us to conclude that the most logical and likely meaning of *malakos* is a man who desires to be penetrated, and not simply a male prostitute. This would be too restrictive in relation to *arsenokoitēs*. In this verse, Paul has simply laid out the active and passive roles in a homosexual act.

> 1 TIMOTHY 1:10 (NAB): [8] We know that the law is good, provided that one uses it as law, [9] with the understanding that law is meant not for a righteous person but for the lawless and unruly, the godless and sinful, the unholy and profane, those who kill their fathers or mothers, murderers, [10] the unchaste, practicing homosexuals, kidnappers, liars, perjurers, and whatever else is opposed to sound teaching,[11] according to the glorious gospel of the blessed God, with which I have been entrusted.

The first thing to consider is the person of the author. The vast majority of exegetes consider that 1 Timothy was not written by Paul. It is not our task to comment on this at this point, but simply to point out the consequences. Either Paul is the author of the epistle, in which case we do not see why *arsenokoitēs* would have a meaning different from that in 1 Cor. 6:9, or the author is different, which would indicate that the negative judgment found in 1 Cor. 6:9 continued in the young Church.[10]

The author invites Timothy to oppose false doctors of the

10. Cf. Gagnon, *The Bible and Homosexual Practice*, 332.

law. He briefly reminds him of the law's function. It is highly likely that the author is not referring to civil law, but to the Mosaic law. Indeed, it would be more than surprising to see the members of the early Church promoting civil law to their community. Moreover "doctors" designate the function of teaching in a religious context, which is that of the young Church. If reference were being here made to civil law, it would be the only mention in the entire New Testament of a specific teaching function of civil law within the heart of the Christian community! This hypothesis is not acceptable. On the other hand, the Mosaic law makes perfect sense. In point of fact, its moral precepts remain valid for the Christian faith. Paul reminds his readers of this in Romans 13:8–9 for example. Moreover, our author states that the law is good, just as Paul did in Romans 7:12, 16. It makes perfect sense to see reference made to doctors charged with teaching the moral precepts of the Mosaic law now adopted by Christianity. Finally, the law's role stands against whatever is opposed to sound teaching. Clearly this refers to religious law. Only the Mosaic law fits these criteria.[11] Our list must therefore be read from this perspective. Consequently, it is logical to read *arsenokoitēs* in the same way as we find it in Lev. 18:22 and 20:13 and to understand it as Paul did in 1 Cor. 6:9.

Conclusion

This study of 1 Cor. 6:9 and 1 Tim. 1:10 legitimately allows us to see in *malakos* the passive partner in a homosexual re-

---

11. Here we are in accord with most commentators of this passage. Only Scroggs refuses to recognize this fact. Is he perhaps influenced by the desire to interpret *arsenokoitēs* from a perspective other than what is found in Leviticus 18 and 20. See his *The New Testament and Homosexuality: Contextual Background for Contemporary Debate* (Philadelphia: Fortress Press, 1983), 118 and 120.

lation and the active partner in *arsenokoitēs*. The judgment Paul has formulated regarding them is clear: they will not inherit the kingdom of God. Paul is talking about acts considered to be most serious, directly offensive to the divine law. This teaching is in line with first century A.D. Judaism. Paul makes no reference to sexual orientation or to specific sexual acts (pederasty, rape, etc.). It is the act itself that is condemned. To say more at this point is impossible.

Letter to the Romans (Rom. 1:18–32)

ROMANS 1:18–32 (NAB): [18] The wrath of God is indeed being revealed from heaven against every impiety and wickedness of those who suppress the truth by their wickedness. [19] For what can be known about God is evident to them, because God made it evident to them. [20] Ever since the creation of the world, his invisible attributes of eternal power and divinity have been able to be understood and perceived in what he has made. As a result, they have no excuse; [21] for although they knew God they did not accord him glory as God or give him thanks. Instead, they became vain in their reasoning, and their senseless minds were darkened. [22] While claiming to be wise, they became fools [23] and exchanged the glory of the immortal God for the likeness of an image of mortal man or of birds or of four-legged animals or of snakes. [24] Therefore, God handed them over to impurity through the lusts of their hearts for the mutual degradation of their bodies. [25] They exchanged the truth of God for a lie and revered and worshiped the creature rather than the creator, who is blessed forever. Amen. [26] Therefore, God handed them over to degrading passions. Their females exchanged natural relations for unnatural, [27] and the males likewise gave up natural relations with females and burned with lust for one another. Males did shameful things with males and thus received in their own persons the due penalty for their perversity. [28] And since they did not see fit to acknowledge God, God handed them over to their undiscerning mind to do what is improper. [29] They are filled with every form of wickedness, evil, greed, and malice; full of envy, murder, rivalry, treachery, and spite. They are gossips [30] and scandalmongers and they hate God. They are insolent, haughty, boastful, ingenious in their wickedness, and rebellious toward their parents. [31] They are senseless, faithless, heartless, ruthless. [32] Although they know the just decree of God that all who practice such things deserve death, they not only do them but give approval to those who practice them.

Multiple Interpretations

The development of the question of homosexuality in the last thirty years has generated all kinds of literature, mostly American, regarding the interpretation of this passage in which homosexual acts are presented as the consequence of God's anger. Faced with a rather crude literal interpretation of this passage, a number of authors have sought to understand this text better by reading it in its historical context. Indeed, although certain Old Testament texts do lend themselves to a discussion of the presence or absence of the theme of homosexuality, this passage from Romans admits of no doubt. All of the authors recognize the Paul that is speaking of at least male homosexuality, and most authors of female homosexuality as well. The question is therefore concretized around the precise nature of this homosexuality and the interpretation that should be given to this passage. This has given rise to a number of often well-researched and highly informed studies.[12] Four lines of interpretation can be seen:[13]

12. For example, B. J. Brooten, *Love between Women: Early Christian Responses to Female Homoeroticism*, Sexuality, History and Society (Chicago-London: University of Chicago Press, 1996).

13. We borrow this classification in part from Gagnon in D. O. Via and R. A. J. Gagnon, *Homosexuality in the Bible: Two Views* (Minneapolis: Fortress Press, 2003), 74–75.

1. Paul does not condemn homosexual relations as such, but rather the exploitation involved in the relations between master and slave, or between young adults (pederasty), or prostitution.[14]

2. Paul had no sense of the notion of sexual orientation. In this passage he is only considering the case of heterosexuals having homosexual relations. One cannot therefore use Romans 1 as an argument to condemn the stable union of two homosexuals.[15]

3. Paul defends the status of the man. According to the model established in the Greco-Roman culture, the man must dominate his sexual partner. Losing this dominating characteristic in the homosexual relation (at least regarding the person who is penetrated), he would lose his dignity. In the same way, female homosexual relations, with one woman dominating the other, challenge this model. This cannot be right. The Apostle therefore opposes these types of relations for this reason.[16]

4. Paul, speaking here of sins committed by pagans in an imaginary dialogue with a Jew, condemns homosexual relations.[17]

For the moment, we do not wish to engage in a detailed discussion with these different authors. Gagnon (in the fourth

14. Cf. R. Scroggs, *The New Testament and Homosexuality*.

15. Cf. D. G. Myers and L. D. Scanzoni, *What God Has Joined Together: The Christian Case for Gay Marriage* (New York: Harper, 2006), 93. See also M. Nissinen, *Homoeroticism in the Biblical World: A Historical Perspective* (Minneapolis: Fortress Press, 1998) and W. Wink, "Homosexuality and the Bible," in *Homosexuality and the Christian Faith: Question of Conscience for the Churches*, ed. W. Wink (Minneapolis: Fortress Press, 1999).

16. B. J. Brooten, *Love between Women*, 359–62.

17. The main representative of this line of thinking in the English-speaking world is R. A. J. Gagnon, *The Bible and Homosexual Practice*, 247.

interpretation) has already questioned the tenets of the three other interpretations, challenging point by point the positions of these other interpreters.[18] The common point of each one of these readings is to interpret the message in favor of or against homosexuality by a close study of terms, having recourse where needed to the historical context, which is sometimes read in such a way as to support the position of the exegete. A detailed study of the use of terms is necessary. Still, this cannot be done without taking into consideration the intention of the author of the biblical text, an intention expressed in the text taken as a whole and not in the particular meaning of each term.

We will begin therefore by looking at an overview of the text in order to determine its meaning in the context of Paul's letter. Only then will we look at the text in more detail. The meaning of the whole will allow us to discern more easily what nuance is to be given to each term and to understand what Paul wanted to say.

Literary Context

A first remark is in order. This text does not have as its primary focus either homosexuality or the morality of it. Rather, it is found within a much larger development beginning with Rom. 1:18 and ending with Rom. 3:20. Homosexual acts are evoked only because they figure in a larger strategy. This needs to be understood before the text is analyzed.

The entire first part of the Letter to the Romans (Romans 1–4) has as its aim to show that justification is achieved by faith and not by the practice of the law. The first step in

18. For Gagnon's arguments against the three other interpretations, see Gagnon, *The Bible and Homosexual Practice,* 347–95.

Paul's argument consists in showing that the divine anger is directed to all of humanity,[19] Jews as well as pagans.[20] Verse 1:18 lays out the thesis that will presented in two steps: a preparatory narrative (1:19–32), which describes the situation of those who commit idolatry, and the body of the argument (2:1–3:18), which, strictly speaking, lays bare the thesis. Verses 3:19–20 form the conclusion.

The preparatory narrative is in the form of a rhetorical speech that has as its aim to anticipate the demonstration. It presents the facts that will enable Paul to make a judgment. He shapes his narrative in such a way as to lay the foundation for his argument. Desirous to show that faith alone leads to justification, Paul begins by evoking the divine anger, a just punishment for human beings' sins. Throughout his missionary career, Paul had to confront those who worshipped in the synagogue about the question of the place of the Mosaic law within the Christian faith. This is why he constructs his arguments for a Jewish audience. He has to show that all are subject to retribution (the divine anger), both Jews and pagans alike, for all are sinners whether or not they are subject to the Mosaic law. This point of view is at first unacceptable to Jewish-Christians. This is why Paul begins by this narrative, constructed from typical points in common in the anti-pagan polemic coming from a Jewish milieu.

It suffices to consider the example of the Letter of Aristeas to Philocratus:[21]

19. God's anger is not a divine punishment external to human beings, but the simple recognition of all of the consequences of their sin.

20. For a more complete study, see J.-N. Aletti, *Comment Dieu est-il juste. Clefs pour interpréter l'epître aux Romains*, Parole de Dieu (Paris: Le Seuil 1991), 54–79.

21. The letter of Pseudo-Aristeas is pseudepigraphal and dates from the

Most other men, in fact, sully themselves by relations between themselves, thus committing a great crime; and entire countries and cities pride themselves because of this; they are not content with relations between males, but they sully their mothers and even their daughters. As for us, we have remained aloof from these vices.[22]

The *Book of Jubilees* (20:5) presents the episode of Sodom as a symbol of the corruption of the pagans.[23] In his *Life of Abraham*, Philo of Alexandria (135–36) condemns homosexual acts because they endanger procreation, but he does not set Jews and pagans directly in opposition to each other.[24] On the other hand, the *Sibylline Oracles* (3:185; 3:595–600) and Flavius Josephus, in his *Against Apion* (2:273–75) are more explicit.[25]

Starting with this stereotypical convention of Judaism, Paul gives the impression to a listener of Jewish origin that he is starting from the listener's point of view. Now, certain details of the text show that Paul is including Jews in this narrative. Let us not forget that Paul wants to show that

first half of the second century B.C. It constitutes the first documentation concerning the origins of the Septuagint (LXX).

22. *Lettre d'Aristée à Philocrate*, number 152, trans. A. Pelletier. Source chrétiennes 89 (Paris: Editions du Cerf, 1962), 175.

23. The *Book of Jubilees* is an apocryphal writing included in the canon of the Ethiopian Bible but not in the Septuagint. This text pretends to present "the history of the divisions of days in the Law, events of years, the years—weeks and the jubilees" such as they would have been revealed in secret to Moses, in addition to the Law, when he remained on Mount Horeb for forty days. *Jubilés, La Bible, Ecrits intertestamentaires*, trans. A. Caquot. La Pléiade (Paris: Gallimard, 1987), 715.

24. Philo, *De Abrahamo*. Introduction, Translation and Notes by J. Gorez in *Oeuvres de Philon d'Alexandrie* 20 (Paris: Editions du Cerf, 1966) 79; or *De Specialibus Legibus* II, 50. Introduction, Translation and Notes by S. Daniel in *Oeuvres de Philon d'Alexandrie* 24 (Paris: Editions du Cerf, 1975) 267 and *De Specialibus Legibus* III, 81.

25. *Oracles Sybillins, La Bible, Ecrits intertestamentaires*, trans. V. Nikiprowetsky. La Pléiade (Paris: Gallimard, 1987) 1062 and 1085. Flavius Josephus, Contre Apion, ed. T. Reinach and L. Blum (Paris: Les Belles Lettres, 1930), 107.

all are subject to the divine anger. In Rom. 1:23, 24, 25, he alludes to Ps. 106:19–20, thereby identifying pagan idolatry with those who worshipped the golden calf at Mount Sinai. It should be noted that Paul does not specify those about whom he is speaking. He is only speaking about "every impiety and wickedness of men" (1:18) and "every form of wickedness" (1:29), calling to mind only actions and not persons. This will allow him in Rom. 2 to explicitly include the Jews among those who are subject to the divine anger.

Paul's originality consists in associating this diatribe against homosexual acts with a criticism of pagan idolatry, which, according to Wisdom 14:2, is the cause of fornication. The connection between these acts and idolatry is one of those points that allows us to understand this passage better.

A Carefully Constructed Argument

Now that we have examined the literary context, we have to try to understand why Paul uses the example of homosexual behavior in his argument. It is in a second step, once the perspective of Paul is known, that we will be able to deepen our understanding of the precise nature of this behavior.

Homosexual behavior is presented as a consequence of human impiety, which is the source of idolatry. The rationale is developed according to a triple repetition of the couplet "human action—divine reaction:[26]

26. We separate verses 19–21 from verse 22 for the following reason: verse 21 developed the question of impiety without touching on the issue of idolatry. This theme will appear for the first time in verse 22. It is impiety that leads to idolatry. There is a logical order between the two and not simultaneity. It is because humans lacked piety that they became idolaters. Now, as we will see, from a theological perspective, homosexuality has a logical link with idolatry. In the same sense, M. J. Lagrange, in his *Epître aux Romains*, Etudes bibliques 27 (Paris: Gabalda, 1916), writes, "This phrase is not linked to the preceding; Paul does not explain what precedes, he points out

verse 18: introduction of the thesis

verses 19–21: the roots of evil: impiety

verses 22–23: human action (idolatry)—verse 24: divine reaction

verse 25: human action (idolatry)—verses 26–27: divine reaction

verse 28a: human action—verses 28b–31: divine reaction

verse 32: conclusion

Each human action repeats the previous one, but with a new form. In the same way, the divine response in verses 26–27 is but a precision of verse 24; verses 28b–31 complement verses 26–27. This construction is interesting from two perspectives. The repetitive character creates an impression of ineluctability, of a state of affairs without a way out—which, as we will see, is related to the meaning of the text. Simultaneously, the variations between steps allow us to establish a parallel between the different expressions thus giving Paul the chance to define the meaning of each one. We also note a strong rhetorical progression, with respect not only to the human action but to the divine reaction as well. The human action moves from the particular to the universal. Paul begins by presenting idolatry in its concrete form, seen in the different animal figures, in order to move to a more general definition in verse 25; he concludes by simply evoking the refusal of a true knowledge of God in verse 28a. To this move toward the universal correspond ever shorter phrases, a stylistic effect that reinforces what he has already said. Greater consequences respond to this progression. In verse 24, Paul speaks only of shameful impurity. In

---

the last degree of error, a veritable stupor, almost madness, accompanied by this supreme illusion that one thinks oneself wise" (p. 26).

verses 26–27, he specifically refers to homosexual acts, and, in verses 28b–31, he expands with a list of vices, beginning with the affirmation that "they are filled with every sort of injustice." From this concentration of style concerning human actions, there is an important development concerning the divine reaction. The list of vices in verses 28b–31 is the longest in Paul's letters!

Paul constructs his argument with reference to four sources:

1. The creation narrative (Gen. 1:26–27).[27] Concerning Gen. 1:26–27, we point out three allusions. The enumeration of "birds, beasts, and reptiles" of Genesis 1 is repeated in a similar way: "birds, four-legged animals, and snakes." The terms "image" and "likeness" are found in Gen. 1:26. The third allusion is to the use of "female" and "male" in Rom. 1:26, 27, used in Gen. 1:27.[28] These allusions are confirmed by reference in 1:20 to the creative act, which forms the background to his argument.

2. What is written in Dt. 4:16–18:

   DEUTERONOMY 4:16–18 (NAB): [16] not to degrade yourselves by fashioning an idol to represent any figure, whether it be the form of a man or a woman, [17] of any animal on the earth or of any bird that flies in the sky, [18] of anything that crawls on the ground or of any fish in the waters under the earth.

   We immediately notice the similarity of language with Gen. 1:26–27. Deuteronomy 4 probably presuppos-

---

27. In his letters Paul frequently refers to Genesis 1–3. Adam is a key figure in his theology (see Rom. 5:12–20; 7:7–12; 1 Cor. 15). His vision of marriage is founded on Gen. 2:4b ff. (see 1 Cor. 6:12–20). There is nothing surprising, then, in his use here of this story of the creation.

28. B. J. Brooten shares this position in *Love between Women*, 240, n. 73.

es Genesis 1. If the greatest similarity of terms between Genesis 1 and Romans 1 allows us to establish a link between these two texts, the influence of Deuteronomy 4 can be inferred by the reference to idolatry, for example.

3. Ps. 106:19–20. We have already pointed out the allusion to this text in Rom. 1:23.

4. The Stoic philosophical tradition. Rom. 1:24–27 contains a number of concepts specific to Stoicism. This has already been pointed out by a number of commentators. Diogenes takes his definition of "passion" (*pathos*) from Zeno, the founder of Stoicism. It is "a movement of the irrational soul and is against nature."[29] Diogenes describes "desire" as an "irrational envy."[30]

Paul's recourse to Scripture structures the argument of these verses, while the use of terms common to the Stoic tradition dresses up the presentation of the verses.[31] We will therefore first consider the role played by the biblical references in these verses before considering our third source.

A Theology of Creation

It is especially interesting to observe how Paul uses his sources and the relationship existing between them. He constructs these verses using the story of creation, the foundation of faith in a creator God. Dt. 4:16 repeats Gen. 1:26, 27,

29. Diogenes Laërce 7:110. *Lives of Eminent Philosophers*, trans. R. D. Hicks (London: W. Heinemann; Cambridge: Harvard University Press, 1958–59).

30. Diogenes Laërce 7:113.

31. This device allows the speaker to gain sympathy for himself from his audience. In effect, to hear from the mouth of his listener terms from his own personal vocabulary rouses sympathy in the listener for someone who shows his vulnerability.

but changes the position of the terms. Gen. 1:26 says "a man according to our image and likeness" and 1:27 specifies "according to our image" with "man and woman." Now in Dt. 4:16 we read: "the form (literally: likeness) of a man or a woman."

Although Rom. 1:23 is closer to Genesis 1 in the choice of terms, we cannot ignore the closeness with Dt. 4:16 from which, it seems, Paul repeats the order in the accusation against idolatry.[32] The result is that humans, when they venerate idols, adore their own image or that of an animal and not God, in whose image they are made.

In Gen. 1:27, God creates humans in his image. Many proposals have been made regarding the nature of this image. In fact, this expression escapes a precise definition because it is polyvalent and complex.[33] Being in the image of God is first of all seen in the invitation to have dominion over the earth. Humans represent God in the created world. This dominion is exercised through fecundity, the fruit of the union between a man and a woman. Without sexual differentiation, dominion would be impossible. Gen. 1:28 makes clear the aim of this differentiation: fecundity, the manifestation of the divine blessing. Dt. 4:16 repeats this differentiation by the adjectives "masculine" and "feminine," without alluding to the finality of this differentiation. Here also, Romans 1 is much closer to the formulation found in Genesis 1 than that found in Deuteronomy 4 but, as in Deuteronomy 4, no allusion is made to fecundity, because homosexual acts are, by nature, sterile.

---

32. A. Pitti, *Lettera ai Romani, nuova versione, introduzione e commento* (I Libri Biblici: Nuovo Testamento 6, Milano: Paoline 2001), 92.

33. Cf. G. J. Wenham, *Genesis 1–15*, Word Biblical Commentary (Waco, TX: Word Books, 1987), 31. For a more complete study, see J.-L. Ska, *Il Libro Sigillato e il Libro Aperto* (Biblica: Bologna, EDB, 2005), 215–23.

Finally, in Gen. 1:26, 28, humans must exercise their dominion over the other creatures: "the birds of the air" and "creeping things." Dt. 4:16 repeats these terms but slightly modifies them: "the form of any bird that flies in the sky." Here again, Romans 1 is, from the point of view of form, closer to Genesis 1 than to Deuteronomy 4. Meanwhile, the notion of dominion found in Deuteronomy 4 is reversed. Creatures are no longer subject to human dominion, but, symbolically, humans are subject to creatures by means of the worship that is given to them.

These three elements allow us to understand why homosexual acts are presented in Rom. 1:23–27 as a consequence of idolatry, while, for the Wisdom tradition, it is only fornication (Wis. 14:12).[34] In Gen. 1:26–27, humans were created to give glory to God and to have dominion over creation. In the case of idolatry, humans are dominated by the creature that they adore; they thereby do not give to the Creator what is uniquely his. There is a reversal of the initial divine project seen, among other ways, in sexual differentiation. In homosexual acts, this differentiation is not considered. This is why for Paul they are the best possible illustration of impiety. This relation between idolatry and homosexual acts is underscored by the use of the verb "to change/to exchange" (*allassō* in Rom. 1:23 and *metallassō* in 1:25, 26, without a perceptible change in meaning).

We are not saying that Paul considers homosexual acts *in se* as the most important of sins. First, this act is merely the consequence of impiety. Idolatry itself is much more serious. Second, we should keep in mind the rhetorical nature of

34. We are indebted here to a note from K. Holter-Stavanger, "A Note on the Old Testament Background of Rom. 1:23–27," *Biblische Notizen* 69 (1993): 21–23.

the argument that Paul is presenting. Homosexual acts are one of the characteristic vices of pagans, according to Jewish tradition. In repeating this tradition, Paul can be assured that he is starting from the furthest point of his Jewish listeners.[35] On the other hand, Paul's use of Genesis 1 and Deuteronomy 4 seems particularly interesting to us as a means of understanding Paul's vision of sexuality. Paul believes that sexual differentiation is willed by the Creator, and that it is a fundamental structure of the human being, a characteristic that is negated in the homosexual act.[36]

What Is Homosexuality?

WHAT IS THE CULTURAL REFERENCE? Now that we have determined the theological (not the moral) orientation of the text, we can now examine more precisely what Paul says about homosexuality in these verses.

First, we have to ask ourselves: what is Paul's cultural reference? In fact, we have uncovered an abundant presence of non-biblical language. Now, the borrowing of vocabulary present in Stoicism, Epicurianism, or other philosophical currents of the first century does not necessarily mean that Paul is repeating the original understanding of the concept. Certain terms could have been conveyed by means of the Greek version of the Old Testament, the Septuagint (LXX), and their meaning could have evolved considerably. It is one thing to say that Paul knew a tradition of thought, either directly by listening to the teachings of the philosophers of Tarsus—an important center of Stoic philosophy—or indi-

35. Whether this listener is real or fictional makes little difference.
36. On the topic of sexual differentiation, it might be interesting to consult the following article: J.-B. Edart, "L'androgyne ou la communion des personnes," *Communio* XXXI 5–6, nos. 187–88 (2006): 83–96.

rectly (by Philo, through the LXX or the Wisdom tradition), and quite another to make of this philosophy or Roman culture the fundamental structure of Paul's thought. The real difficulty lies in the just evaluation of the place occupied by each one of Paul's sources. Given Paul's faith and his education in pharisaism, we should be justified in finding there the main basis of his thought. Whatever influence may have come from the Greco-Roman culture needs to be integrated in his faith. Because his Judeo-Hellenistic background does not allow us to give a satisfactory account of an expression, it would be correct to take into consideration the more specifically pagan culture.[37] Now that we have spelled out these preliminary considerations, we can examine each of the expressions found in Paul and attempt to understand just what kind of behavior Paul is referring to when he affirms in Rom. 1:26–27:

> ... females exchanged natural relations for unnatural, and the males likewise gave up natural relations with females and burned with lust for one another. Males did shameful things with males and thus received in their own persons the due penalty for their perversity.

HOMOSEXUALITY AND NATURE. Before asking ourselves the meaning of the concept of nature and the expressions derived from it, we need to answer two questions. Paul clearly speaks about homosexual acts between males in 1:27, but what about women in 1:26? Strangely enough, we find no term expressly designating the homosexual act. Paul uses only paraphrases. Because of this, some rare exegetes see in 1:26b not a lesbian relationship, but the choice of cer-

37. In Rom. 7:15b–19, we have a clear reference to Medea of Euripides. Cf. J.-B. Edart, "De la necessité d'un sauveur, Rhétorique et théolgie de Rm 7, 7–25" in *Revue biblique* 105 (1998): 380–82.

tain women to engage in oral or anal sex with a male partner.[38] The parallel construction between 1:26b and 1:27a, where homosexual relations between men is not in doubt, allows us to relativize this rather marginal interpretation. Paul himself highlights this construction by the use of the word "likewise." Paul is certainly referring to both male and female homosexual acts. When introducing acts between women, he does not limit himself to sodomy but also takes into consideration every act performed between women.

The second question concerns the meaning of the word "exchange" as in "females exchanged . . . ." This question may seem strange, given the obvious meaning of the word. Still, according to certain authors, this exchange means that Paul is referring to heterosexuals having homosexual relations. As a consequence, according to these same authors, persons with an innate homosexual orientation do not fall into the category under consideration by Paul.[39] The phenomenon of an exclusive attraction for the same sex was known in antiquity. In the absolute, Paul could have made this distinction, but two arguments refute this position. First, certainly Paul could have made this distinction, but precisely he did not! It is always methodologically doubtful to have recourse to an argument from silence. Second, our text is not a description of homosexuality as such. Rather, homosexuality is placed in a theological context already

38. See J. Miller, "The Practices of Rom. 1:26: Homosexual or Heterosexual?" *Novum Testamentum* 37 (1995): 1–11. According to Miller, the rarity of sources referring to female homosexuality in the ancient world makes it difficult to imagine that Paul could have been considering this or even imagine it. For a complete response to Miller see B. J. Brooten, *Love between Women*, 248, n. 99. Brooten gives other examples of interpretation in the same line as Miller.

39. Cf. J. Boswell, *Christianity, Social Tolerance, and Homosexuality: Gay People in Western Europe from the Beginning of the Christian Era to the Fourteenth Century* (Chicago: University of Chicago Press, 1980), 109.

mentioned. Paul's interest in homosexual acts is their logical relationship to idolatry. Paul underscores this by his repetition of the same verb "exchange" in 1:25 and 26 and by his use of "change" in 1:23, which has exactly the same meaning as the preceding verb. It is clear therefore that Paul is not interested in the question of the sexual orientation of persons. Rather, the act in and of itself is under consideration, because of its symbolic significance.

Exegetes interested in the question of homosexuality raise questions about the exact nature of these relations which are "against nature." The answer to this question is found in the correct understanding of the term "nature" and the expressions that are derived from it. Ancient authors give different meanings to this concept according to the culture to which they belong. The adjective "natural" could characterize acts in accord with the social conventions of a particular group, as in the case of a legislative body.[40] Thus in the Greco-Roman culture, the relationship between dominant and dominated, rather than that between male and female, established the moral norm. A sexual relation was "against nature" if it did not respect this norm. In a married couple, the man was the dominant one, and a relationship in which he lost this position was considered to be "against nature," for it did not respect this fundamental structure of the cosmos which ordained the superiority of the male.[41] This is why in

40. See Artemidorus, *Onirocritica* 1:78–80. Artemidorus is an author from the second century A.D. For more information see B. J. Brooten, *Love between Women,* 175–86.

41. For a detailed presentation of this, see the well-researched article by R. B. Ward, "Why Unnatural? The Tradition behind Romans 1:26–27," *Harvard Theological Review* 90 (1997): 263–84. The author presents the story of *Timaeus* in which Plato explains the first generation of humans was made up only of men. It was not until the second generation that men who had lived cowardly lives were reincarnated as women (90e or even 42a–b, where Plato says that human nature is double: the superior one being called man

imperial Rome, the union of a master with one of his slaves was not considered to be "against nature." If the master dominated his slave, he respected the social structure. On the other hand, if he was dominated by the slave, then the sexual relation would be "against nature," for it would not be in conformity with social norms. A lesbian relationship was always "against nature" because the woman exchanged her passive and submissive role for one that was dominant and active. Relying on this reality, a whole current of North American authors[42] has asserted that we must understand Paul in this sense because he belonged to a Greco-Roman culture.

That Paul was directly confronted with the Greco-Roman culture, no one would deny; that it was a part of his cultural background is undeniable fact. But it would be necessary to balance this affirmation against the Judeo-Hellenistic dimension of Paul's culture.

In the writings of Paul himself we find statements that are hardly compatible with this Greco-Roman vision of sexuality. In 1 Corinthians 7, the rights of the spouses over the body

[anēr]). The man who does not succeed in mastering his body with its pleasures would assume the inferior nature of a woman (eis gynaikos physin) at the second birth (genesis).

42. M. Nissinen, *Homoeroticism in the Biblical World*, 57–88. This author integrates in his vision the theory of "gender," a category developed in the United States in 1955 and that authors of the gay culture use quite readily, for it allows them to distinguish sex (biological) from "gender" which would be the "social" sex chosen by the person: "Clearly, a 'natural' relation implies not only a difference of *gender* and the complementarity of the sexes, but also *gender roles. . . . Gender role categories* are not determined by the anatomical sex, but by a presentation of oneself appropriate to and in conformity with the roles of the established gender" (107); D. Swancutt, "'The Disease of Effemination': The Charge of Effeminacy and the Verdict of God (Rom. 1:18–2:16)," in *New Testament Maculinities*, Semeia Studies, ed. S. D. Moore, J. A. Anderson (Society of Biblical Literature, 2003), 192–233. B. J. Brooten, *Love between Women*, 241. It is interesting to note that Brooten recognizes in a note (n. 75) that if the penetration of a man of an inferior social status was seen as natural in the Greco-Roman world, this was not the case in Leviticus. Alas, this does not justify his choice to have the pagan background predominate over the Jewish one.

of the other are strictly reciprocal and equal.[43] We cannot deny that Paul, while maintaining the equality and dignity of the man and the woman, attributes to each one a specific vocation and role within the couple. He does not hesitate to affirm in 1 Cor. 11:3 that the man is the head (in the sense of "head", or "origin") of the woman and for this reason the wife should not bring shame on her husband, but should be his glory. In the story of Gen. 2:18–25 to which Paul refers in 1 Cor. 11:7–12, the wife is the glory of the husband in the precise sense that she honors him.[44] She is his joy and a source of his pride because of the irreplaceable complementarity that she brings to him. This complementarity is translated by the famous play on words between *ish* for the man and *ishah* for the woman in Gen. 2:23. The woman will be the glory of God in seeking to be, as far as possible, the glory of the man. This complementarity, stemming from Gen. 2, is found in 1 Cor. 11:11–12. Concerning the honor that the husband can find in his wife, we read in Prov. 11:17: "A gracious woman wins esteem, but she who hates virtue is covered with shame."

The context of Rom. 1:19–23 also invites us to see in this nature the order willed by God and seen in his creation. From this perspective, "against nature" can legitimately be understood with reference to Genesis 1 repeated in 1:20–24,

43. The negative view of sexuality goes back to Tertullian and St. Jerome, and has since been projected back onto St. Paul, who does not share their negative views. Another interpretation, suggested by Origen and enjoying a comeback in the last thirty years, sees Paul's famous statement of 1 Cor. 7:1, "it is not good for a man to touch a woman," as a quotation by Paul of a statement contained in the letter sent by the Corinthians to Paul. Paul follows with his own comments about this statement. This interpretation and the positive vision of sexuality that flows from it, cohere much better with 1 Cor. 6:20: "Glorify God in your body." If sexual intercourse were a lesser evil, a sin that was permitted, 1 Cor 6:20 would be incomprehensible.

44. See A. Feuillet, "L'homme 'gloire de Dieu' et la femme 'gloire de l'homme' (1 Co XI: 7b)," in *Revue biblique* 81 (1974): 161–82.

which presents a clear vision of the man-woman structure in the act of creation. God desired sexual union between the man and the woman, and this divine will or divine law is inscribed in nature. We can observe this by means of all of the elements that characterize sexual identity, genitalia being one of the principal signs. This also is what is suggested in verses 19–20. Rom. 1:26–27 is clearly speaking about homosexual relations (between women and between men). They are called "against nature" because they are contrary to the plan of the Creator since they "unite" two people of the same sex. If we want to take into consideration the Roman meaning of this term (that which is natural respects social convention), we could say that an act "against nature" does not respect the social convention established by God in creation.

A DRAMATIC ILLUSTRATION. Having established the precise nature of homosexual acts, we can now look at Paul's moral judgment on them. They are qualified as "against nature," a property touching on the essence of this behavior. Moreover, the tripartite structure (human action–divine reaction) and the repetition that results from it, place in parallel three expressions that characterize homosexual acts and their consequences in a more precise way. In verse 24:

> Therefore, God handed them over to impurity through the lusts of their hearts for the mutual degradation of their bodies.

In verses 26–27:

> Therefore, God handed them over to degrading passions. Their females exchanged natural relations for unnatural, and the males likewise gave up natural relations with females and burned with lust for one another. Males did shameful things with males and thus received in their own persons the due penalty for their perversity.

In verse 28:

> And since they did not see fit to acknowledge God, God hand-
> ed them over to their undiscerning mind to do what is im-
> proper.

An analysis of these expressions allows us to give substance
to the meaning of homosexual acts from a theological perspective, according to Paul, and their consequences on humans. We believe it possible to synthesize them in the following three points: the loss of freedom, the lack of respect
for the body, and the blindness of the conscience.

THE LOSS OF FREEDOM. We have examined the careful construction of our text using the triple repetition of the schema
human action–divine reaction. This is expressed by the triple repetition of the verb "hand over." This translates the action of God in verses 23, 24, and 26. God hands them over
to impurity, to their passions, to their undiscerning minds.
God posits a positive act. Before looking more closely at the
nature of this act, it will be helpful to consider the human
act, or rather the attitude that is the source of this act. Indeed, at each step of his analysis, Paul refers us back to an
interior attitude. In verse 24, it was through the lust of their
hearts that they were handed over to impurity. In verse 27,
men burned with lust for one another. In verse 28, they are
handed over to their undiscerning minds. Here we have the
only reference in all of Scripture to the interior dimension
preceding homosexual acts. This interior dimension seems
clearly to be the source of these acts. This clearly shows that
assent to desire is part of the moral act and that it, too, is
subject to condemnation.

How are we to understand the divine action? In what does
it consist? In his *Homilies on the Letter to the Romans* (3:3),

John Chrysostom understands here that God "allows."[45] He abandons them "so that having experienced the object of their desires, they will hide themselves out of shame."[46] Paradoxically, the verb "allow," which expresses the divine action, means that humans are fully responsible for their actions, echoing the inexcusable character of the initial fault pointed out in verse 20. Therefore Paul offers us a humanity fully responsible for its acts.

Through the use of the verb "hand over," we can also see that humans are deprived of their freedom, being slaves to their lusts. In fact, "hand over," which can be used in the sense of giving a gift to someone, expresses the idea of being at the disposal of something or someone. This is the reason why this verb is used frequently with reference to the passion of Christ both in the New Testament and in Paul's letters.[47] This verb is used twice in order to convey the fact that a person, excluded from the Christian community, is handed over to Satan. In 1 Cor. 5:5 we read that "such a man be handed over to Satan";[48] in 1 Tim. 1:20, we read: "I handed them over to Satan."

Returning to Rom. 1:18–32, we understand how this drama found in Rom. 7:14–20 can shed light on the person chained by passions. He discovers, like the unnamed person in Romans 7,[49] an internal power that dominates that place where he thought he could exercise his freedom. The wage

45. Cf. PG 60:414.   46. PG 60:415.

47. Cf. Rom. 4:25; 8:32; Gal. 2:20; Eph. 5:2, 25.

48. Having been excluded from the community, the ostracized Christian is seen as no longer being protected from the power of Satan.

49. Rom. 7:7–12 presents us with a monologue in the first person singular by one who is not immediately identifiable. It cannot, in fact, be Paul. A number of proposals have been made over the course of the history of the interpretation of this passage. See C. E. B. Cranfield, *The Epistle to the Romans*, Vol. 1. International Critical Commentary (Edinburgh: T & T Clark, 1974), 344.

received as a consequence of the error in Rom. 1:27 appears logically as God's abandonment of this person, who is handed over to the power of sin.[50] God's anger is not a punishment coming from the outside, but quite simply the exposure of all of the consequences that flow from a refusal of God and his mercy. In the realm of sexual sin, this leads to dishonoring the body, to the loss of control over one's impulses. Paul explicitly mentions this loss of control: "males ... burned with lust for one another." Unless we have recourse to elements not found in the text (venereal disease, feminizing of the appearance, which was a source of humiliation in Roman society, and so forth), this is the only hypothesis suggested by the text.

THE LACK OF RESPECT FOR THE BODY. In the second verse, Paul speaks of "degrading passions." This expression echoes that found in verse 24: "degradation of their bodies." To degrade one's body is not readily understood today. It is important to understand precisely what Paul means here and, in a larger sense, the semantic meaning of this expression.

"Passion" is a word rarely found in Paul. It occurs only three times (Col. 3:5; 1 Thess. 4:5; Rom. 1:26). In Col. 3:5 Paul writes: "Put to death, then, the parts of you that are earthly: immorality, impurity, passion, evil desire, and the greed that is idolatry." Impurity and fornication refer to the sexual sphere. The Greek word that translates "passion" cannot simply mean "passion" or "affection." The context clearly indicates erotic passion.

The passions are called "degrading, "dishonorable." 1 Thess. 4:3–5 has an interesting take on this:

50. Gagnon, *The Bible and Homosexual Practice*, 261.

This is the will of God, your holiness: that you refrain from immorality, that each of you know how to acquire a wife (*skeuos*)[51] for himself in holiness and honor, not in lustful passion (*pathos*) as do the Gentiles who do not know God . . .

The similarity of this teaching to Rom. 1:18–32 is clear. We find the same connection between a lack of knowledge of God and sexual immorality. The opposition between "holiness and honor" and "lustful passion" echoes the expression "degrading passions" of Rom. 1:26. Paul underscores the positive value of sexuality. It is excess born of a disordered passion, the fruit of lust, that is condemned. Inasmuch as the body is a sexual one, it is seen as an essential element for the sanctification of humans. It is an instrument of holiness and must therefore be respected. In 1 Cor. 6:20, Paul does not hesitate to call to mind that the body is a temple of the Spirit, and he invites Christians to glorify God in their bodies, that is, in the right exercise of sexuality.

The only possible referent in Romans 1 is the first story of creation, whose traces we have already pointed out. The person can either honor or dishonor the body. The man and the woman, in the physical manifestation of their sexual being, have a dignity, a particular honor. The dignity of the body is linked to its capacity to show forth the union be-

51. There is a lot of discussion involving the meaning of *skeuos*. Literally, it means "vase." This could be a metaphor referring to one of three possibilities: wife, a man's body, the man's genitals. For a complete study, cf. S. Légasse, *Les Epîtres de Paul aux Thessalonicens*. Lectio Divina 7 (Paris: Les Editions du Cerf, 1999), 209–22; to be complemented by A. Tosato, "I primi richiani di Paolo in tema matrimonial (1 Ts 4, 3–8)," in *Studi sul Vicino Oriente Antico didicati alla memoria di Luigi Cagni*, ed. S. Graziani, Dipartimento di Studi Asiatici, Series Minor 61 (Naples: Istituuto Universitario Orientale, 2000), 1–26. The latter shows, in the light of the Qumran texts—which have not until now been taken into consideration—that Paul is making reference not to the conjugal act, but rather to the juridical conditions of marriage.

tween the man and the woman, to express physically this "being in the image of God." In the homosexual relation, the dimension of the body is contradicted. The body, the symbol and place of the union between the man and the woman, becomes a sign of their lack of union.

MORTAL BLINDNESS. In the third affirmation, persons are handed over to their "undiscerning minds." The Vulgate, translating *sensum* instead of *mentem*, was sensitive to the fact that *nous* (mind, intelligence) does not simply mean speculative reason, but the moral faculty at the origin of a moral action.[52] The choice of this expression is tied to a play on words with "calculate, judge" (*dokimazō*) in the first part of the verse. Humans did not judge rightly (*edokimasan*) and that is why they are handed over to their "undiscerning" (*adokimon*) minds. This rhetorical figure underscores the connection between the refusal to know God and the consequent loss of moral judgment. The adjective *adokimos* means "inept," "disqualified." It shows that the refusal of the knowledge of God makes reason lose all credibility. Here Paul repeats verse 21, where he states that "they became vain in their reasoning, and their senseless minds were darkened." This darkening of the moral faculty finds expression in the proliferation of vices.

Rom. 1:32 brings to a conclusion this third step of the cycle begun in 1:22. Paul alludes to 1:28 by the use of the word "know" which takes us back to "knowledge." He explains the exact meaning of "undiscerning mind." Those described know the "decree of God," what has been prescribed by God. Here it concerns a law established by God which is known

52. M. J. Lagrange, *Romains*, 31.

not simply by means of the intellect. As we know, *epignōsis*, which is used here, means something different from *gnōsis*, intellectual knowledge. It is a knowledge implying the integration of the known object into the moral life. Here, it means that humans also know the threat of death associated with different vices.[53] This death sentence is not to be understood as the same thing as a juridical death sentence. Rather, it must be understood in an eschatological sense. These works lead to eternal death, to the definitive separation from God.

Does Paul Condemn Homosexual Acts?

In his study of the narrative texts, Innocent Himbaza concludes saying, "In order to know if the Bible says anything regarding homosexual relations, the reader must turn to other texts of the Old Testament such as the legislative passages in Leviticus or, in the New Testament, to the writings of Paul." The time has come to respond to this delicate question. An examination of 1 Cor. 6:9 and 1 Tim. 1:10 allows us to state that Paul and the author of 1 Timothy consider homosexual acts to be contrary to the law of the Gospel. This is confirmed in the study of Rom. 1:18–32, even if, as we have already said, Paul's primary intention in these verses is not to formulate a moral judgment on homosexual acts.

If Paul situates what he says about homosexual acts in a rhetorical perspective whose end concerns justification by faith, this should in no way lessen the importance of what he has to say concerning homosexual acts. We must simply be attentive to take into consideration his judgment on ho-

53. M. J. Lagrange, *Romains,* 34.

mosexual relations and the emphasis used to strengthen his reasoning.

We have been able to establish that Paul considers sexual relations between members of the same sex (be they men or women) to be counter to the project of God as seen in creation. For this he makes use of Genesis 1 and its application to idols in Deuteronomy 4. His position is perfectly in harmony with the Judaism of his time. His originality is in the relationship he establishes between idolatry and homosexual acts. Both are inversions of God's will for his creatures.

The rootedness in the divine intention manifested in creation and seen in the sexed nature of human persons (both corporeal and spiritual) is, in itself, the answer to three of the four positions taken at the beginning of this study. The first states that Paul is dealing only with a certain type of sexual relation, seen in the exploitation of the weak by the strong. If the condemnation of homosexual acts is based on a theology of creation, there can no longer be forced relations, which would be condemnable, or chosen relations, which would be acceptable. All homosexual acts are against nature, that is, opposed to the divine will, whether they be between men or between women. Moreover, beyond this argument, nothing in the text supports the thesis that Paul is talking about sexual relations imposed by force. It is clearly stated that women exchange their natural relations for those that are against nature, the same as for men. The text underscores the free initiative of persons handed over to their passions by God. The precision that Paul brings to bear on this exchange shows that the point of the text is between a heterosexual relation, which is natural, and a homosexual relation, which is against nature.

The second position turned on Paul's ignorance of sexual orientation in order to affirm that only bisexual relations were condemned. Here again, beginning with the origins of humanity, Paul destroys this argument. Homosexual acts remain against nature, whether they are experienced by someone with a heterosexual orientation or by a person with a homosexual orientation within the confines of a stable affective relation.[54]

The third position invoked the Greco-Roman cultural context as means of understanding "against nature" as opposed to conventions. In fact, Paul would have liked to safeguard the typical machismo of the surrounding pagan culture! Once again, Paul's recourse to the stories of the origins invalidates this hypothesis. Paul finds his moorings in his spiritual heritage. The sameness of vocabulary with that of the ambient culture is, at best, only one of the elements of his rhetorical strategy.

The last position sees in our text a condemnation of homosexuality. This statement must be nuanced, since homosexual acts are not the main concern of Rom. 1:18–32.[55] Moreover, homosexuality as a psychological state is not condemned. It is only homosexual acts and the desires at their origin that are condemned. As is the case for all moral behavior, the distinction between the persons and their acts is essential here. Homosexuality is a psychological reality that can give rise to certain kinds of affective or sexual behaviors. A psychological reality that does not result in behavior is not subject to moral judgment. Only acts and desires to which one fully consents can be qualified as good or evil.

54. B. J. Brooten, who defends the third position, rightly notes: "The distinction between sexual orientations is clearly an anachronism that does not assist in understanding Paul's line of argument" (*Love between Women*, 242).

55. Gagnon is clear on this point. It is simply the wording that is unfortunate.

For Paul, the point of reference is the divine law.[56] Every act that is opposed to the divine precepts is evil and worthy of condemnation.

Jesus

The Healing of the Slave (Lk. 7:1–10)

> LK. 7:1–10 (NAB): [1] When he had finished all his words to the people, he entered Capernaum. [2] A centurion there had a slave who was ill and about to die, and he was valuable to him. [3] When he heard about Jesus, he sent elders of the Jews to him, asking him to come and save the life of his slave. [4] They approached Jesus and strongly urged him to come, saying, "He deserves to have you do this for him, [5] for he loves our nation and he built the synagogue for us." [6] And Jesus went with them, but when he was only a short distance from the house, the centurion sent friends to tell him, "Lord, do not trouble yourself, for I am not worthy to have you enter under my roof. [7] Therefore, I did not consider myself worthy to come to you; but say the word and let my servant be healed. [8] For I too am a person subject to authority, with soldiers subject to me. And I say to one, 'Go,' and he goes; and to another, 'Come here,' and he comes; and to my slave, 'Do this,' and he does it." [9] When Jesus heard this he was amazed at him and, turning, said to the crowd following him, "I tell you, not even in Israel have I found such faith." [10] When the messengers returned to the house, they found the slave in good health.

THE FAITH OF THE CENTURION. Jesus' exclamation in verse 9 indicates to the reader Luke's intention to highlight the faith of the centurion. The story is constructed around this figure. The officer never appears in person in the story but always through representatives: first, the elders of the syn-

56. See, for example, Rom. 13:8–10, where the entire law is summed up in the commandment of love.

agogue, then some friends. This allows Luke to underscore the greatness of his faith and humility.

It is said that he sent elders of the Jews to Jesus. This fact is interesting. The centurion does not himself go to him. The sending of a delegation can be explained by his awareness of the fact that Jews and pagans should not come into contact with each other. Wishing to respect this law, the soldier sends others to represent him. We can see here an indication of the delicateness of heart of this knowledgeable pagan who admired Jewish customs. The elders' words support the consistency of this hypothesis: "He deserves to have you do this for him, for he loves our nation and he built the synagogue for us." He is thus presented to us as a friend of Israel. His love for Israel has even led him to build a synagogue. We see the same attitude in the person of another centurion, Cornelius, in Acts 10:2: "devout and God-fearing along with his whole household, [he] used to give alms generously to the Jewish people and pray to God constantly." In both instances, Luke strongly underscores their attachment to Israel, an attitude of heart that predisposes them to hope for salvation. In the first story, this is realized in the healing of the slave; in the second, by baptism of the entire household.

This attitude of heart of the officer is again illustrated in the second half of the story. While Jesus proceeds with the elders toward the house, friends of the soldier come to Jesus with a message. The centurion tells Jesus not to come under his roof because he is not worthy, but if Jesus will simply say the word, his servant will be healed. His confession of unworthiness echoes the words of the elders who proclaimed his worthiness.

The figure of the centurion is consistent with the whole

of Luke's gospel, where openness to the salvation of all nations is one of the principal themes. The centurion's faith allows salvation to enter into his house, a reality seen visibly in the healing of the slave. This wonderful pagan figure is an example of Christian behavior in his relationship to the Lord. He is humble; he has complete confidence in the saving power of God and he believes without seeing. Perhaps we can add to this Luke's desire to remind Christian converts from paganism the debt they owe to Israel.[57]

THE SLAVE AS OBJECT OF ATTENTION. The figure of the slave is presented using two substantives: "slave" (*doulos*) and "servant/child" (*pais*) with the qualification "valuable" (*entimos*). In Luke's narrative strategy, this adjective explains the centurion's concern for his servant. What, precisely, does *entimos* mean? The Vulgate translates it by *pretiosus*, that is, "precious," the early meaning of *entimos* (cf. Is. 13:12: "I will make mortals more precious than pure gold, men more precious than gold of Ophir"). This exception does not exclude the possibility that the slave was precious in an affective sense. Thus the humanity of the owner is underscored. The adjective qualifies the slave, but from the point of view of the narrative, it qualifies the principal protagonist: the centurion. It is not possible to be more precise about the nature of this relation on the basis of the few elements we have in the text. None of the elements chosen by Luke in the construction of this story allows us to be more specific about the nature of their affective relationship.

---

57. G. Rosse, *Il Vangelo di Luca, comment esegetico e teologico*, 3rd edition (Rome: Città Nuova Editrice, 2001), 250.

CONCLUDING REFLECTIONS. Some authors have seen in the attachment of the centurion to his slave the sign of a homosexual relation.[58] Jesus' attitude is therefore understood as welcoming of this relationship. The problem is first of all hermeneutical. An important principle in the writing of biblical texts is that of economy. The hagiographer says only what is needed to express the message to be conveyed. The result is that to read a biblical text requires that one asks about what is being said and not about what is not said, unless the silences are part of the narrative strategy or the discourse which then requires proof.

Now, Lk. 7:1–10 does not in any way allow us to pronounce on Jesus' attitude toward homosexuality. This can only be a strictly ideological reading, based on the projection of preconceived ideas. This story simply has as its aim to underscore the beauty of the centurion's faith, the proof of which is an active charity toward a man for whom society does not have the least esteem. This text shows us that faith leads the Christian to abolish all boundaries (here social) between people and to believe that the saving power of Christ can bring together each one in his or her poverty, whether it be physical, moral, psychic or social.

The Beloved Disciple

An expression might lead some people to believe that one of Jesus' disciples could have been a homosexual: "the beloved disciple." This expression occurs several times: in Jn. 13:23 during the Last Supper, in 19:26 at the foot of the Cross, in 20:2, 8 when the tomb was found to be empty and in 21:7, 20 at the appearance of the resurrected Jesus on the shore

58. D. A. Helminiak, *Ce que la Bible dit vraiment de l'homosexualité*, trans. D. Gille (Paris: Le Seuil, 2005), 196–200.

of Lake Galilee. He is also called "the other disciple" in Jn. 18:15–16 and 20:2–8.

The strongest passage to express this relation between Jesus and the anonymous disciple is Jn. 13:22–26:

> JN. 13:22–26 (NAB): [22] The disciples looked at one another, at a loss as to whom he meant. [23] One of his disciples, the one whom Jesus loved, was reclining at Jesus' side. [24] So Simon Peter nodded to him to find out whom he meant. [25] He leaned back against Jesus' chest and said to him, "Master, who is it?" [26] Jesus answered, "It is the one to whom I hand the morsel after I have dipped it." So he dipped the morsel and (took it and) handed it to Judas, son of Simon the Iscariot.

There are two elements that, for a modern mind, could be ambiguous: one is a name, the other is a gesture. Let us begin with the gesture since the name deserves to be treated in all of its occurrences.

RECLINING AT TABLE! The expression is made up of a verb "recline" (*anakeimai*) and a clause that can be translated literally "in the breast of Jesus" (*en tō kolpō tou Iēsou*). The verb is used frequently to describe the manner in which guests usually reclined around the table: Jn. 6:11: "Then Jesus took the loaves, gave thanks, and distributed them to those who were reclining (*anakeimenois*), and also as much of the fish as they wanted"; or again, in Jn. 12:2: "They gave a dinner for him there, and Martha served, while Lazarus was one of those reclining at table with him."[59] The same is found in the other gospels as well, for example, in Mt. 9:10: "While he was at table in his house, many tax collectors and sinners came

59. It would be more correct, in a translation more concerned with the meaning of the expression than with a word for word translation, to render the text by "he was at table with him."

and sat with Jesus and his disciples." Thus this verb has no affective and, even less, sexual connotation to it.

The clause merely describes the position of the disciple, reclining at Jesus' side with his head at the level of Christ's chest. This can be verified in verse 25 when, questioned by Peter, the disciple must lean his head back to ask his master. The position leads him to lean his head to the level of his chest. Nothing here indicates in any way an erotic dimension. To assert otherwise is to make the text say more than it does. It is also to forget the economy of the text. The author judges it good to underscore here the proximity between Jesus and this disciple at a dramatic moment: Judas' betrayal.

It is not without reason that the he repeats here for the only time the term "chest" (*kolpōs*) that had been used in Jn. 1:18 and which characterizes Christ's relationship with the Father: "The only Son, God, who is at the Father's side, has revealed him." He thus suggests that the intimacy between this disciple and Jesus is bound to be the same as the intimacy that exists between the Son and the Father. This theme will be developed in the notion of divine sonship: to be son in the Son. This remark leads us to an understanding of the expression "beloved disciple." He is the one who lives in God and God in him, just as the Word lives in the heart of the Father. The Christian is called to live from the communion that exists in the Trinity.

A MODEL DISCIPLE. A large number of studies have been done on this mysterious designation, and we are unable to discuss them all here.[60] Once again, the principle of economy must be taken into consideration. The end of the gospel

60. For a more precise analysis, see A. Marchadour, *Les personages dans l'évangile de Jean. Miroir pour une christologie narrative*, Lire la Bible (Paris: Editions du Cerf, 2004), 169–80, or E. Cothenet, *La chaîne des témoins*

identifies this disciple as the author of this book (Jn. 21:21–24). He therefore voluntarily maintains his anonymity, never using the first person singular in his writing and referring to himself only through Jesus' attitude toward him. This point is essential if we are going to judge the meaning of this designation at its true value. We must first place ourselves on the level of the act of reading. This distancing by the author concerning himself allows us to create a space in which the reader is invited to enter in order to identify him or herself with this exceptional disciple.[61]

Beyond the symbolic meaning, we can certainly perceive a historical reality in our expression. It suffices to point out that this disciple appears at key moments. Thus he has a privileged place within the divine plan. Still, he is not the only one loved. It is sufficient to recall Jesus' friendship with Lazarus and his sisters, Martha and Mary (Jn. 11:5). Jesus says that he loves his disciples with the same love as the Father (Jn. 15:9). Jesus' love is not exclusive. How, then, are we to understand this particular choice?

The beloved disciple is the one who in Jn. 21:22–23 is invited to live on, a rather remarkable phrase in John's gospel. Jesus says to the Jews: "If you remain in my word, you will truly be my disciples" (Jn. 8:31). The beloved disciple thus represents the one who, from the beginning, had been the perfect disciple.[62] This explains why he received Christ's confidence on the evening of the last supper, why Mary was entrusted to his care, and how it was that he immediately believed on seeing the empty tomb. Christ's preferential love

dans l'évangile de Jean. De Jean-Baptiste au disciple bien-aimé, Lire la Bible (Paris: Editions du Cerf, 2005), 123–36.

61. L. Devillers, "Les trios témoins, une structure pour le quatrième évangile," Revue biblique 104 (1997): 179–80.

62. A. Marchadour, Les personages dans l'évangile de Jean, 179–80.

can be explained not by a particular friendship based on personal attraction but by the total commitment of a man on the way that Jesus has come to reveal.

To conclude, we can state that to see a homosexual relation between the "beloved disciple" and Jesus is simply another example of an ideological reading of a biblical text. If a preference could exist between Jesus and this man, nothing in the text permits us to see in this preference a homosexual relation. This preference could simply express an exceptional commitment on the part of this disciple, making him a model for all future disciples.

Jesus and Homosexual Acts

HE WHO SAYS NOTHING CONSENTS. We have seen that the gospels do not allow us to say that Jesus shows the least approval of homosexual acts. He says and does nothing explicit on this subject. The only way allowing us to interpret with precision this silence is to refer to his immediate cultural background: first-century Judaism. Now we have seen how Judaism judges homosexual acts as being contrary to God's Law, basing itself as much on the commandments of Leviticus as on the story of Sodom and Gomorrah. Jesus did not controvert this teaching, even though he did not hesitate to reject other points (see Mt. 23 and Mk. 7). Jesus' silence on this matter can only be interpreted as reflecting agreement with the tradition of Israel on this point. Besides, it is highly probable that he never directly came across this question in the Jewish milieu, since, given the existing prohibition, this behavior had no social visibility.

JESUS AND HUMAN LOVE. Jesus' position on homosexuality can also be deduced from his discourse on human love.

We have echoes of this each time he speaks of marriage. In Mt. 19:1–9 and Mk. 10:1–12 he deals with the question of divorce. Beyond the differences in approach between the two texts, we can adduce that Jesus refers explicitly to Gen. 1:27 and 2:24 by his repetition of "from the beginning" (Mt. 19:4) and "from the beginning of creation" (Mk. 10:6). This reference to the beginning and the will of the Creator shows that Jesus sees heterosexual relations as willed by God. We recall the theology of Romans 1. We do not need to develop an entire exegesis of this text in order to understand that Jesus belongs to the strictest Jewish legal tradition regarding divorce. Dt. 24:1–4 permits divorce in the case where the husband finds "something shameful" (*'erwat dâbâr*) in his wife. The Jewish tradition of the first century discussed the nature of this "shameful thing." The school of Hillel does not hesitate to say that a bad meal was enough, while the school of Shemmaï at least required sexual immorality.[63] The exception introduced by Mt. 19:9 (except for "immorality") shows that Jesus is in the line of Shemmaï and even goes beyond it.[64] Suffice it to say that such a position is incompatible with any kind of acceptance of homosexuality as a possible model of human love willed by God!

The Commandment of Love

We may wonder if the commandment of love of neighbor (Mk. 12:30–31) does not imply refraining from judging others' behavior and even more so when it comes to a non-chosen sexual orientation or a choice for homosexual love.

It is impossible to consider only one text. For example,

---

63. Mishna, *Gittîm* 9:10.
64. We will not enter into a study of this Matthean exceptive clause with its legendary difficulties, as it is useless for our discussion.

we could limit ourselves to a study of the Good Samaritan, but this parable does not take into account the question of the commandment of love. Here we come to the heart of the matter. In fact, Jesus states that he came "not to abolish but to fulfill the law" (Mt. 5:17). The law is unambiguous concerning homosexual acts. Jesus himself observed the commandments, and so he took pains to teach his disciples what relationship to maintain with the law and God's will. Would the commandments of the Old Covenant be in contradiction with the commandment of love of the New Covenant? Do all of the commandments depend on the commandment of love?

THE FULFILLMENT OF THE LAW. Matthew 5–7 presents a deep reflection on the relationship to the law. Matthew's gospel, whose audience was very probably Jewish in origin, had to respond to the question on the relationship to the law. Jesus illustrates the fulfillment of the law by using six examples, beginning with: "You have heard it said . . . but I say to you." The fulfillment of the law is brought about, etymologically speaking, by radicalizing it, that is, by returning to the root or the essence of the law. This is not a negation of the formal commandments but the call to a more demanding following of them.

In his controversies with the Pharisees, who were very attached to the teaching of the elders, Jesus reproaches them for having abandoned God's law: "You disregard God's commandment but cling to human tradition" (Mk. 7:8). Using the example of ritual purity, the source of numerous washings of plates, Jesus teaches his disciples the nature of true filth for the human heart. It is not what enters by the mouth, but evil thoughts arising from the heart that corrupts human beings: "From within people, from their hearts, come evil thoughts, unchastity, theft, murder, adultery, greed, malice, deceit, licentiousness,[65] envy, blasphemy, arrogance, folly" (Mk. 7:21–22).

Jesus took liberties with some of the commandments—for example, healing on the Sabbath in the synagogue. He never did this to challenge the law itself. His "infractions" always serve a prophetic function: to announce the coming of the kingdom. The Sabbath finds its fulfillment in Jesus; this is why it no longer has a *raison d'être* ("the Son of Man is Lord of the Sabbath" [Mt. 12:8]). The same holds true for laws dealing with worship. The temple is no longer the place of the divine presence. The risen Christ is the new temple. Laws permitting admission to worship and governing it are now de facto null and void. There is no longer ritual impurity.

The commandment to love others does not therefore abolish all of the old law; rather, it transforms it by penetrating deeper. Jesus states that the law depends on two commandments: love of God and love of neighbor (Mt. 22:40). The law finds its meaning, its deep structure, in charity. Individual commandments are the expression of charity. Thus there is no contradiction between commandment and love, but rather a necessary connection. The law is subject to love, but love finds expression in the law.

LAW AND MERCY. We have briefly mentioned Jesus' presence among sinners. Having established that the commandment of love serves to integrate the commandments of the second tablet of the law, we can look at Jesus' attitude in his relations with sinners, a particular expression of the love of neighbor. Because we are examining the theme of sexuality, let us

65. In Greek, *porneia*. This expression refers implicitly to all of the commandments in Leviticus 18–20, and therefore to homosexual acts.

look at two episodes in which Jesus encounters "sexual" sinners: the adulterous woman (Jn. 8:1–11) and the forgiven sinner (Lk. 7:36–50). We cannot examine the entirety of each of these rich and complex stories, but will limit ourselves simply to Jesus' attitude regarding the sin of the person.

In Jn. 8:1–11, a woman caught in the very act of adultery is brought to Jesus by some scribes and Pharisees. They demand his opinion on the death penalty prescribed by the law for this kind of transgression. Jesus invites the one who is without sin to throw the first stone, and then he pretends to ignore them by writing on the ground. Caught in a trap, the accusers depart, leaving Jesus alone with the woman. His attitude with respect to her is summarized in one question and two affirmations: "Woman, where are they? Has no one condemned you?" "Neither do I condemn you" and "go, and sin no more" (Jn.:11).

Jesus begins by underscoring the lack of condemnation. The first word is one of mercy. Then he sends the woman away, telling her to sin no more. By this last word, Jesus implicitly formulates a judgment on the act of adultery. Nonetheless, this judgment is formulated in such a way as to prolong the word of mercy. Jesus denounces the sin without accusing the sinner and invites her to live uprightly according to the forgiveness that he has given her.

In Lk. 7:36–50, the evangelist recounts the story of a woman, probably a prostitute, weeping at Jesus' feet and wiping them with her hair during the course of a meal given by a Pharisee. This story illustrates what Jesus said in the preceding section. Jesus defines himself as the friend of sinners (Lk. 7:34) and made a distinction between, on the one hand, the publicans and the people, justified and, on the other hand, the Pharisees and scribes who have rejected God's plan. In our story, the "righteousness" of the Pharisee is an obstacle that keeps him from receiving salvation.

A careful reading of the story reveals a certain number of tensions that point to an important work of composition. The aim is to emphasize the contrast between the sinner and the Pharisee in order to highlight the message of this passage. Jesus is invited to dine at the home of a Pharisee, a normal custom after the preaching of a visiting rabbi to the synagogue. A woman, a sinner, pours a vase of perfume on the feet of the Master. Her whole attitude betrays her humility and her veneration of Jesus. The act of untying her hair in front of another man was enough for a husband to divorce his wife, according to certain rabbinical texts. She hides nothing of her sinful state before the Master. Jesus' attitude is disconcerting. He lets her do it, quietly accepting these marks of esteem. The Pharisee respects the rules of hospitality by saying nothing, but the narrator tells us this: Jesus cannot be a prophet for, normally, Jesus is not clairvoyant like a prophet.

Jesus responds with a little parable revealing that he knows the interior judgment of the Pharisee. This revelation of hidden thoughts allows the narrator to point out that Jesus is indeed a prophet since he knows hidden thoughts! We see at one and the same time Jesus' delicacy with respect to his host. He does not directly reproach his rash judgment. We also see the mild irony directed to the reader since the Pharisee is condemned by his own thoughts. Jesus' response also reveals that it is with full knowledge of the facts that he allows himself to be touched by the woman.

The parable does not address the problem of ritual purity, which was a pharisaical concern, but rather interprets the conduct of the woman. Her behavior is presented as the fruit of the forgiveness she has received. Let us note in passing that Jesus recognizes the greater justice of the Pharisee as compared to the woman: his debt is ten times less. Still, he also reveals that God shows himself to us as a God of forgiveness. This truth reverses the situation and makes the sinful woman superior to the Pharisee, for she knows something that he does not. By his question, Jesus invites his host to realize that the sinful woman has had an experience that he has not yet had: the personal experience of God's goodness to him. From this experience, the woman has received a capacity to love which is the sign and consequence of a forgiveness already received. Jesus, as prophet, knew that, beyond her sin, her heart was capable of love. Having received the approval of the Pharisee, Jesus could focus his attention on the woman and her behavior. He describes in detail the woman's gestures. She performed the traditional gestures of hospitality from a host, things that the Pharisee did not do. While the Pharisee calls the woman a sinner, Jesus shows him the love that dwells in her heart. The contrast between the woman and the Pharisee could not be more complete.

Verse 47 spells out the conclusion. All the same, the reader may be surprised by it. We would have expected to read: "the person to whom much has been forgiven, loves much; the one to whom little has been forgiven, loves little." Only the second part of the verse corresponds to this logical conclusion. According to the first part of the verse, the love shown by the woman is the cause of the divine forgiveness. How are we to understand the tension between these two propositions? We are probably seeing here some redactional traces; Luke, wishing to add an exhortation: the forgiveness received remains operative if it is maintained out of a true love. We find an echo of this notion in the Lord's Prayer:

"and forgive us our sins as we ourselves forgive everyone in debt to us" (Lk. 11:4). The story ends with the words of the pardon that, according to the logic of the parable, has already been received. Verse 50 indicates the new interior state created by the act of faith in Christ's saving power: "Go in peace!" This peace is not a psychological reality in Scripture, but the full realization of the promises of salvation for the sinner.

Nothing in this story permits us to say that Jesus approves of or ignores the woman's sin. On the contrary, her sin is fully taken into consideration; without it, there would be no sense in accepting her gestures of thanksgiving. At the same time, we notice Jesus' extreme tact, not only toward the woman but toward the judgmental Pharisee as well. No one is accused directly. Once again, as in Jn. 11:8, the denunciation of sin is included in the act of forgiveness and is therefore preceded by it.

We chose two texts that dealt with sexual issues. We could also have examined the story of Zacchaeus (Lk. 19:1–10). This story deals with a social issue: stealing as an abuse of the public trust. Our conclusion would have been the same. Jesus does not accuse Zacchaeus, but he merely says at the end of the story: "Salvation has come to this house" (Lk. 19:9). This word necessarily implies, a fortiori, the denunciation of Zacchaeus's sinful behavior, without which, what does salvation mean?

Does this imply that the accusation of sin and judgment is contrary to the Gospel? For those who know the biblical texts, the answer is obvious. It suffices here to recall the text on fraternal correction or Jesus' accusation against a generation that seeks signs. That generation is called "evil" (Lk.11:29–30). The words spoken to the Pharisees in Mt. 23:23 are even more explicit: "You serpents, you brood of vipers, how can you flee from the judgment of Gehenna?" These commandments are directed precisely at those who are convinced that they are just. On the contrary, confronted with the sinner who repents, mercy does not linger on the sin but it immediately gives the hoped-for forgiveness and restores the person in his or her dignity.

We can conclude this section on the relationship between the law and mercy by affirming that there is no opposition between the two. Quite the contrary. The exercise of mercy presupposes the existence and the goodness of the law. It is in fact its very condition. "For judgment is merciless to one who has not shown mercy; mercy triumphs over judgment." Why? Because it has anticipated and not ignored it!

Conclusion

The principal danger of every study of texts on this subject is to project the current situation. In his introduction to this book, Innocent Himbaza has rightly defined the necessary distinction "between homophilia or homophobia, on the one hand, and, on the other hand, biblical teaching on sexual behavior of which homosexuality may be a part." We are not proposing a modernization of these texts, but a synthesis of the message that their human authors wished to convey. Even if the stories of the Old Testament do not provide a clear judgment on homosexual acts, and even if the full weight of the commandments of Leviticus can appear to be limited by their context, still, the texts of the New Testament and, particularly the apostle Paul, are much more clear.

Paul

The two references in 1 Cor. 6:9 and 1 Tim. 1:10 speak about the active and passive partners in a homosexual act. Saint Paul clearly pronounces a moral judgment on those who commit such acts: they cannot enter the kingdom of God. This radical condemnation is quite in keeping with the Jewish tradition and shows continuity with the Old Testament texts on this subject. The neologism *arsenokoitēs*, the most probable source of which is Lev. 18:20, confirms this. As Adrien Schenker has stressed, this re-use also indicates that the Torah has a meaning that goes beyond the primary one willed by the human author. The law is perceived in its divine origin and not in the limits of its historical genesis.

The Letter to the Romans uses the example of this sexual behavior to illustrate the consequences of the refusal to recognize the Creator. Paul does not describe the reality of homosexuality, but his argument leads him to reveal the theological significance of it. It is characterized as being "against nature," that is, contrary to the will of the Creator as it is manifested in sexual differentiation. It is interesting to note that Paul considers female homosexuality, the only reference to it in all of Scripture. This confirms what Schenker said concerning the extension of the commandment of Leviticus 18 to women.

We must point out that, if homosexuality finds itself under a microscope, it is because it serves the purposes of a much larger argument. Paul presents a bleak picture of the human condition in order show what kind of situation humanity finds itself in when it refuses God. In the same vein, the condemnations put forth in 1 Cor. 6:9 and 1 Tim. 1:10 are integrated into lists of vices that function hortatively. This should lead us, not to deny the judgment that Paul makes, but to avoid using the same style when speaking specifically about homosexuality. The apoditic character of the divine Law must not be separated from the numerous texts in which Paul emphasizes the superabundance of the divine mercy and even makes himself an ambassador of it.

We can affirm that in Paul's writings homosexuality is not perceived as a psychological reality but rather is perceived from the perspective of the symbolic and theological meaning of homosexual acts. Paul's approach is rooted in a much larger vision of human sexuality. What is needed for completion of this study is a deeper analysis of those texts that deal more directly with sexuality, such as 1 Corinthians 6:12–20 and 1 Corinthians 7. The reference to the creation story is the foundation of the universal character of Paul's judgment. According to him, it is applicable to all people at all times.

Jesus

The study of the gospel texts leads us to dismiss any reading that sees in this story or that expression an allusion to homosexuality. On the contrary, the few texts that touch on the question of sexuality in the teaching of Jesus clearly indicate that he understands the story of Genesis 2 as normative for human love.

The same can be said with respect to the relationship between love and mercy. To rely on the commandment of love to justify complacency regarding profoundly rooted behaviors in the person, as in the case of homosexuality, is contrary to gospel teaching. If Jesus shows great freedom with respect to the law, this touches only those commandments whose validity ends with his coming—for example, worship and ritual purity. Elsewhere he reaffirms the permanent validity of the Decalogue and takes no liberties with the moral law. On the contrary, the study of Matthew 5–7 shows that Jesus went to the root of the law's demands. Charity is presented as the soul of the entire law and finds its full expression in the truth.

This charity finds its highest expression in mercy, a reality seen in the story in John 8 of the adulterous woman and in the story from Luke 7 of the sinful woman who washed Jesus' feet and was forgiven. Jesus' tact when faced with repentant sinners does not even lead him to evoke the law. The sinner's attitude already witnesses to the fact that he or she is known and accepted.

Conclusion

Now that we have completed these three studies, it is time to offer a brief synthesis of the results and to show their possible points of contact. Each author studied the texts for himself. Now it is time to try to answer the question: "What does the Bible say about homosexuality?"

Synthesis of the Results

The Stories of the Old Testament

Innocent Himbaza began his study with an analysis of Genesis 18 and Judges 19. These two stories underscore the importance of the crime committed by the inhabitants both of Sodom and of Gibeah: hospitality is not respected, the foreigner is not welcomed. This is the principal message of these texts for Israel.

These stories include another element: it is the male travelers who are the object of the men's lust, not women. These stories take into account the fact of homosexuality present both in Israel and in the neighboring populations. Homosexuality is seen exclusively as a limited behavior and not as a psychological state. These acts are grave, being qualified as "madness/infamy." They are clearly evaluated negatively. Still, Himbaza rightly points out that the context of violence does not permit us to take into consideration the case of a relation based on mutual and free consent between the two partners.

In a second stage, our author dealt with the interpretation made by some regarding the story of the friendship between Jonathan and David. He clearly shows that this relation between the two men is not a homosexual one. A good understanding of the expressions in their literary and historical context, at first ambiguous to the modern reader, do not allow us to project onto these texts a vision that is foreign to them. The relationship between Saul's son and the future king of Israel is that of a political alliance and not an erotic one.

Leviticus

In an original and innovative study, Adrien Schenker shows why Leviticus forbids homosexual relations. They endanger family cohesion by introducing into it a love relation different from that which structures the family ties. This conclusion is particularly interesting. Many authors dealing with this subject question the specific evaluation of these acts as "an abomination to the Lord." They look for the value this expression gives to the prohibition. Schenker, taking account of the immediate context, succeeds in uncovering the meaning of the prohibition in this particular setting: the protection of the family.

These two passages consider the individual less than the good of the family. In their estimation, homosexual acts would weigh too heavily on a human community already exposed to a number of dangerous pressures.

A homosexual relation is seen as dangerous for the cohesion and peace of a large household in which several generations, several wives of the same husband, several children

born from different women, several adult males in a sub-
ordinate position or several bosses working together in the
family business, must live together and get along with each
other. In this setting, a homosexual relation between men
would complicate even more the delicate preservation of a
harmonious equilibrium between all.

This analysis of the two prohibitions against homosexual relations between men, both in their own context and in
light of the conclusions of these two chapters (Lv. 18:24–30
and 20:22–24), clearly shows the importance that is attached
to them. These are not ritual commandments of minor significance. From the perspective of the family highlighted by
our author, homosexual acts are clearly condemned. This
judgment will leave its mark on the entire Jewish tradition
up until Paul.

The New Testament

Certain gospel stories have been subjected to the same kind
of projection as the story of Jonathan and David. Jean-Baptiste Edart's analysis has shown that the expression "beloved
disciple" is a technical term used by John to give a place to
the Christian reader in the biblical story. That this is based
on a special friendship between Jesus and one or another of the apostles has no homosexual connotation at all; no
trace of it can be found in the texts. The same thing can be
said for the story of the healing of the centurion's slave in
Luke 9. Neither the customs of the time, nor the qualification of "dear" or "precious" with respect to the slave, allows
us to see in this text the least allusion to a homosexual relation. No passage in the gospels allows us to justify the least
indulgence on Jesus' part toward homosexuality. On the other hand, a reflection on the relationship between law and

love underscores how quickly Christ's mercy manifests itself, and this regardless of persons or their sins. The stories of the woman taken in adultery and that of the weeping sinner, both of whom committed sexual sins, illustrate Jesus' merciful consideration for all sinners of contrite heart.

The texts of the Apostle to the Gentiles are sufficiently delicate to have generated an abundant literature in the debate on homosexuality. As a matter of fact, several statements are particularly strong. 1 Cor. 6:9 and 1 Tim. 1:10 speak about the passive and active partners in a homosexual relationship. Certain interpretations succeed in giving another meaning to the words used only by means of a convoluted analysis in which probability places a key role. This is understandable in light of Paul's cutting and uncompromising judgment: "They cannot enter the Kingdom of Heaven." The literary genre of these passages is not able of itself to explain this judgment. It is negative. This negativity is apparent also in Rom. 1:18–32. These verses, the beginning of a much broader argument on justification, take up a theme common to the Jewish tradition, viz., that homosexuality is a characteristic behavior of pagans. In the only such instance in all of Scripture, Paul makes reference to lesbian relations. He situates himself in the line of the Jewish tradition rooted in Leviticus 18 and 20. His use of *arsenokoitēs*, a neologism found in Leviticus 18 and 20, indicates the importance of these texts. Still, and rather surprisingly, Paul does not explicitly base the justification of his position on these passages from the Torah. Rather, he refers to the Creator and his work. Homosexual acts are called "against nature," that is, opposed to the Creator's will. They are the concrete illustration of the fact that humans have turned from their origins in order to fall down prostrate before idols. It is important to point out that Paul's perspective is theological. He is interested in the meaning of homosexual acts within the divine plan.

What Does the Bible Say about Homosexuality?

The Biblical Data

To inquire of the Bible as Bible implies a recognition of the unity formed by all of these books together. We inquire of *the* Bible as one book. This view is not simply tied to faith in the inspired character of this writing. The human authors of each book frequently take up earlier biblical writings. The work of redaction of certain books points to the fact that the authors themselves were aware of the unity of the whole.

This internal cohesion is seen in a convergence between the different texts analyzed. The texts of the Old Testament already formulate, explicitly or implicitly, a negative moral judgment on homosexual acts. Even if the stories of the book of Genesis or of Judges have the question of hospitality as their first aim, homosexuality is an aggravating factor in the crimes committed. Leviticus finds itself in a similar situation. Beyond the historical context, homosexual acts are characterized as an abomination before the Lord. By means of the Torah and Jewish tradition, the apostle Paul makes the same judgment and uses it in his argument in Romans and in his list of vices. It seems difficult to avoid the conclusion that the Bible never approves of homosexual acts: they are against the will of God the Creator. The modern reader should keep in mind that we are dealing with theological texts and so they should be interpreted from that perspective. Still, we should point out that through the figures of David and Jonathan, or of Christ and the beloved disciple, the Bible takes a very positive view of friendships between two men.

How to Interpret This for the Modern World

Given all of this, we must ask ourselves what value this judgment has for today's world. Two arguments could be obstacles to a possible use of the biblical judgment in the contemporary context.

The first obstacle is tied to how the biblical authors perceived homosexuality. This has already been discussed; what is clear is that they did not understand homosexuality as a psychological reality identified by a sexual attraction for persons of the same sex. Biblical language is very concrete. The texts that we have studied only consider homosexual acts between men or between women. It is the sexual act that is considered. Still, it would be naïve to think that a simple attraction has no place. If homosexual relations are a danger to family unity in Leviticus, this implies that they are also viewed from the affective standpoint and not simply the genital. This can be verified in St. Paul. The Letter to the Romans emphasizes the role of desire as a source for acts that are against nature. The developments on sexuality in 1 Corinthians 6 and 7 and Ephesians 5 allow us to understand that sexuality is always seen as an attraction and a love relationship between a man and a woman. The fact that homosexuality is not understood in the Bible in the same way as it is today takes nothing away from the judgments found in it. Even if the notion of tendency, the fruit of development in psychology of the last century had not yet been developed, the reality is certainly present.

The second argument that could lead to casting doubt on the pertinence of the Bible's moral judgment in today's world is the contextual nature of these writings. They were written in very precise historical contexts that are no longer necessarily pertinent today.

The example of Paul's teaching on the subject provides an interesting answer to this subject. In effect, Paul repeats the traditional Jewish teaching on the law as expressed in Leviticus. He also bases himself on the theology of the creation as an expression of the divine will. The first point attests to the fact that, beyond the detailed dimensions of these writings, Paul values them because they express the divine will. It would be a mistake to think that Paul interprets the law while ignoring the context of these Old Testament writings. Paul simply does not take them into consideration, for the circumstances surrounding a biblical writing take nothing away from its value as an inspired text. For example, this can be seen in the gospels and Paul's letters from the end of the first century to the beginning of the second century. The first community after the apostolic period does not ignore the reasons that led the evangelists and Paul to write what they did. It does not prevent this community from recognizing them as inspired and normative for their faith and their moral and ecclesial life. The inspired character of the biblical writings gives these texts a perennial value to what is formed by and in history. The interpretation will consist then in defining how the teaching is brought up to date in a historically defined form. Paul's interpretation, with the entire Jewish tradition of Leviticus, is an example of this process. The historical context has changed, but what has been set forth remains valid. Schenker shows clearly how an accurate understanding of the context of the writing allows for nuancing—for example, the death penalty, a formulation designed more to highlight the seriousness of the offense than actually to be imposed.

A second element allows us to understand what weight is to be given to Paul's teaching. Paul uses a theology of creation to justify his judgment. In so doing, he expands his judgment beyond the Covenant and its Law. Thus Paul makes it clear that his message is valid for all of humanity and at all times. It would be erroneous to ignore the value of this analysis for our own day, under the pretext that Paul's teaching is the product of a particular historical context. Paul's intention is clearly universal. This fact contradicts any position that would affirm that sexual acts have no moral value in themselves without reference to the life of the person, to cultural constructs, and to circumstances. If such were the case, forms of sexuality that are considered aberrant (incest, pedophilia, bestiality, etc.) would likely be recognized one day as good if they corresponded, for example, to the cultural constructs of the day!

Question for Today

For the purpose of updating this teaching in today's world, we would like to ask a question and issue an invitation. The question is one asked by Adrien Schenker in his conclusion. He asked if the public recognition of homosexuality did not contribute to the fragmentation of an already fragile society. He expanded on this question by asking if Leviticus 18 and 20 do not invite us to consider sexuality as much from a personal point of view as to the point of view of the community. This question appears to us to be especially timely if we take into consideration the place occupied by the family in the Semitic world during this period of history. The family was a microcosm of society. Indeed, although the large cities allowed for an intermingling of different families, this was not the same in rural areas. Marriages often occurred within the same clan, between cousins broadly speaking. We can affirm that the family identified itself with the society. As a consequence, a contemporary reflection that wishes to take into consideration the contribution of biblical revelation cannot afford to ignore this given.

To conclude our study, we wish to invite our readers not to stop their study at what Scripture says about homosexuality. Indeed, each one of us will have noticed that this subject, so present in the current social debate, occupies only a minimal place in Scripture. If we felt the need to spend a long time on this subject in this book, it is because it seemed important to bring clarity to this issue, given the impact of this question in today's world. On the other hand, Christ's invitation to recognize his merciful love can be found on each page of the New Testament! It is in the light of this call to live by mercy that we need to hear Christ's teaching on human love.

Bibliography

Aletti, J.-N. *Comment Dieu est-il juste. Clefs pour interpréter l'épître aux Romains.* Parole de Dieu. Paris: Le Seuil, 1991.

Anderson, A. A. *2 Samuel,* Word Biblical Commentary 11. Dallas, TX: Word Books Publisher, 1989.

Artémidore. *Onirocritica,* 1.78–80.

Bailey, K. "Paul's Theological Foundation for Human Sexuality, 1 Cor 6,12–20 in the Light of Rhetorical Criticism." *Near East School of Theology Theological Review* 3 (1980): 27–41.

Barthélemy, D. *Critique textuelle de l'Ancien Testament,* 1. *Josué, Juges, Ruth, Samuel, Rois, Chroniques, Esdras, Néhémie, Esther.* OBO 50/1. Fribourg, Suisse: Éditions Universitaires; Göttingen: Vandenhoeck & Ruprecht, 1982.

Bosman, T. "A critical review of the translation of the Hebrew lexeme אהב." *OTE* 18 (2005): 22–34.

Boswell, J. *Christianity, Social Tolerance, and Homosexuality: Gay People in Western Europe from the Beginning of the Christian Era to the Fourteenth Century.* Chicago: University of Chicago Press, 1980.

Boven, F., and P. Geoltran, eds. *Écrits apocryphes chrétiens I.* Paris: Gallimard, 1997.

Briend, J. "Les figures de David en 1 S 16,1–2S 5,3. Rapports entre littérature et histoire." In *Figures de David à travers la Bible,* XVII congrès de l'ACFEB (Lille, 1–5 septembre 1997), edited by L. Desrousseax and J. Vermeylen, 9–34. Lectio Divina 177. Paris: Éditions du Cerf, 1999.

Brooten, B. J., *Love between Women: Early Christian Responses to Female Homoeroticism, Sexuality, History and Society.* Chicago/London: University of Chicago Press, 1996.

Campbell, A. F. *I Samuel.* FOTL 7. Grand Rapids, MI/Cambridge, U.K.: William B. Eerdmans, 2003.

Caquot, A., and Robert P. De. *Les livres de Samuel.* CAT VI. Geneva: Labor et Fides, 1994.

Cothenet, É. *La chaînes des témoins dans l'évangile de Jean, De Jean-Baptiste au disciple bien-aimé.* Lire la Bible. Paris: Éditions du Cerf, 2005.

Cranfield, C. E. B. *The Epistle to the Romans,* vol. 1, ICC. Edinburgh: T & T Clark, 1974.

Cross, F. M., D. W. Parry, R. J. Saley, and E. Ulrich. *Qumran Cave* 4 XII 1–2 *Samuel.* DJD XVII. Oxford: Clarendon Press, 2005.

Devillers, L. "Les trois témoins, une structure pour le quatrième évangile." *RB* 104 (1997).

Dhorme, P., *Les livres de Samuel.* Études Bibliques. Paris: Gabalda, 1910.

Dickson, P. "Response: Does the Hebrew Bible Have Anything to Say about Homosexuality?" *OTE* 15 (2002): 350–67.

Douglas, M., "Justice as the Cornerstone: An Interpretation of Leviticus 18–20." *Interpretation* 53 (1999): 345–47.

Dupont-Sommer, A., and M. Philonenko, eds. *La Bible. Écrits intertestamentaires.* Paris: Gallimard, 1987.

Edart, J.-B. "De la nécessité d'un sauveur. Rhétorique et théologie de Rm 7,7–25." *RB* 105, (1998): 380–82.

Egelkraut, H. *Homosexualität und Schöpfungsordnung. Die Bibel gibt Antwort.* Vellmar-Kassel: Verlag Weisses Kreuz GmbH, 1993.

Feldman, L. H. "Josephus' Portrayal (Antiquities 5.136–174) of the Benjaminites Affair of the Concubine and Its Repercussions (Judges 19–21)." *JQR* 90 (2000): 255–92.

Feullet, A. "L'homme "gloire de Dieu" et la femme "gloire de l'homme" (1 Cor XI, 7b)." *RB* 81 (1974): 161–82.

Gagnon, R. A. J., *Homosexuality in the Bible: Two Views.* Minneapolis: Fortress Press, 2003.

———. *The Bible and Homosexual Practice: Texts and Hermeneutics.* Nashville, TN: Abingdon, 2001.

Grundmann, W. *Das Evangelium nach Lukas.* Berlin, Berlin: Evangelische Verlangsanstalt, 1963.

Helminiak. D. A. *Ce que la Bible dit vraiment de l'homosexualité.* Translated by D. Gille. Paris: Les empêcheurs de tourner en rond–Le Seuil, 2005.

Himbaza, I. "Israël et les nations dans les relectures de Juges 19, 22–25: débats sur l'homosexualité." Forthcoming.

Holter, K. "A Note on the Old Testament Background of Rom 1, 23–27." *BN* 69 (1993): 21–23.

Horner, T. *Jonathan Loved David: Homosexuality in Biblical Times.* Philadelphia: Westminster Press, 1978.

Jobling, D., *The Sense of Biblical Narrative: Three Structural Analysis in the Old Testament (I Samuel 13–31, Numbers 11–12, I Kings 17–18). Journal for the Study of the Old Testament* 7 (1978).

Josèphe, F. *Contre Apion.* Edited by T. Reinach and L. Blum. Paris: Les Belles Lettres, 1930.

——. *Les Antiquités juives,* vol. I, livres I à III. Text, translation, and notes by É. Nodet. Paris: Éditions du Cerf, 2000.

——. *Les Antiquité juives,* vol. II, livres IV et V. Establishment of the text, translation, and note by Étienne Nodet. Paris: Éditions du Cerf, 1995.

Koch, T. R. "Cruising as Methodology: Homoeroticism and the Scriptures." In *Queer Commentary and the Hebrew Bible,* edited by K. Stone, 169–80. *Journal for the Study of the Old Testament* 334. Sheffield: Sheffield Academic Press, 2001.

Lacoque, A. "Abomination." *Dictionnaire encyclopédique de la Bible.* 3 éd. revue et augmentée. Published under the direction of Centre Informatique et Bible, Abbaye de Maredsous. Turnhout: Brepols, 2002.

Lagrange, M. J. *Épître aux Romains.* Études Bibliques 27. Paris: Gabalda, 1916.

Lanoir, C. *Femmes fatales, filles rebelles: Figures féminines dans le livre des Juges.* Actes et Recherches. Geneva: Labor et Fides, 2005.

Lefebvre, P. "David et Jonathan: un homme rencontre un homme." *La vie spirituelle* (2001): 199–214.

——. *Livres de Samuel et récits de résurrection. Le messie ressuscité "selon lex Écritures."* Lectio Divina 196. Paris: Éditions du Cerf, 2004.

Légasse, S. *Les Épîtres de Paul aux Thessaloniciens.* Lectio Divina, commentaires 7. Paris: Éditions du Cerf, 1999.

Lettre d'Aristée à Philocrate. Trad. A. Pelletier, Sources Chrétiennes 89. Paris: Éditions du Cerf, 1962.

Lewis, T. J. Art. "Belial." In *ABD* 1, 654–56.

Lust, J., "David dans la Septante." In *Figures de David à travers la Bible,* edited by L. Desrousseaux and J. Vermeylen, 243–63.

Mackensie, S. L. *Le roi David: Le roman d'une vie.* Essais bibliques 38. Geneva: Labor et Fides, 2006.

Marchadour, A. *Les personnages dans l'évangile de Jean: Miroir pour une christologie narrative.* Lire la Bible. Paris: Éditions du Cerf, 2004.

Mccarter, P. K. *I Samuel: A New Translation with Introduction and Commentary.* Anchor Bible 8. New York/London/Toronto/Sydney/Aukland: Doubleday, 1980.

Michaelis, J. D. *Abhandlung von den Ehegesetzen Mosis welche die Heyrathen in die nahe Freundschaft untersagen* 2, und vermehrte Aufl. Göttingen: Abraham Vandenhoeck's seel. Witwe, 1768.

Milgrom, J. *Cult and Conscience. The* Asham *and the Priestly Doctrine of Repentance.* Studies in Judaism in Late Antiquity 18. Leiden: Brill, 1976.

―――. *Leviticus* 17–22: *A New Translation with Introduction and Commentary.* Anchor Bible 3A. New York/London/Toronto/Syndey/Aukland: Doubleday, 2000.

Miller, J. "The Practices of Romans 1, 26: Homosexual or Heterosexual?" *NT* 37 (1995): 1–11.

Myers, D. G., L. D. Scanzoni. *What God Has Joined Together: The Christian Case for Gay Marriage.* New York: HarperSanFrancisco, 2006.

Nissinen, M. "Die Liebe von David und Jonathan als Frage der modernen Exegese." *Bib* 80 (1999): 250–63.

―――. *Homoeroticism in the Biblical World: A Historical Perspective.* Minneapolis: Fortress Press, 1998.

Oracles sybillins. La Bible, Écrits intertestamentaires. Translated by V. Nikiprowetsky. La Pléiade. Paris: Gallimard, 1987.

Peleg, Y. "Love at First Sight? David, Jonathan, and the Biblical Politics of Gender." *JSOT* 30 (2005): 171–89.

Philon d'Alexandrie. *De Abrahamo.* Introduction, translation and notes by J. Gorez. Œuvres de Philon d'Alexandrie 20. Paris: Éditions du Cerf, 1966.

―――. *De Specialibus Legibus I et II.* Translated by S. Daniel. Paris: Éditions du Cerf, 1975.

―――. *De Specialibus Legibus III et IV.* Translated by A. Mosès. Paris: Éditions du Cerf, 1970.

Pitta, A. *Lettera ai Romani, nuova versione, introduzione e commento.* I Libri Biblici, Nuovo Testamento 6. Milan: Paoline 2001.

Pope, M. H. "Homosexuality." *IDBSup,* 415–17.

Römer, T., and L. Bonjour. *L'homosexualité dans le Proche-Orient ancien et la Bible.* Essais bibliques 37. Geneva: Labor et Fides, 2005.

Rosse, G. *Il Vangelo di Luca, commento esegetico e teologico.* Rome: Città Nuova Editrice, 2001.

Schenker, A. "Der Monotheismus im ersten Gebot, die Stellung der Frau im Sabbatgebot und zwei andere Sachfragen zum Dekalob." In A. Schenker, *Text und Sinn im Alten Testament, Textgeschichtliche und bibeltheologische Studien,* 188–92. OBO 103. Göttingen: Vandenhoeck & Ruprecht, 1991.

―――. "Propheten schon vor Mose und Esras Verbot der Mischehen, zwei ungelöste Probleme im Esrabuch." In *Studien zu Propheten und Religionsgeschichte,* edited by A. Schenker, 132–39. Stuttgarter biblische Aufsatzbände, A.T. 36. Stuttgart: Kath. Bibelwerk, 2003. Also available as "A causa da crise dos casamentos mistos em Esdras, uma nova explicacão." In *Utopia urgente* (Mélanges offerts à J. C. Pinto de Oliveira), edited by F. Betto, A. Bezerra de Menezes, and Th. Jensen, 419–27. São Paulo: Casa Amarela educ, 2002.

———. "What Connects the Incest Prohibitions with the Other Prohibitions Listed in Lev 18 and 20?" In *The Book of Leviticus: Composition and Reception,* edited by R. Rendtorff and R. A. Kugler, 162–85. FIOTL 3; VT.S 93; Leiden/Boston: Brill, 2003.

Schroer, S., and T. Staubli. "Saul, David und Jonathan—eine Dreiecksgeschichte? Ein Beitrag zum Thema "Homosexualität im Ersten Testament." *BK* 51 (1996): 15–22. Also available as "Saul, David and Jonathan—The Story of a Triangle? A Contribution to the Issue of Homosexuality in the First Testament." In *Samuel and Kings,* edited by A. Brenner, 22–36. A Feminist Companion to the Bible (Second Series). Sheffield: Sheffield Academic Press, 2000. Also available as "'Jonathan aima beaucoup David.'" L'homoérotisme dans les récits bibliques concernant Saül, David et Johathan." *Foi et Vie* 94 (CB 39) (2000): 53–64.

Scroggs, R. *The New Testament and Homosexuality Contextual Background for Contemporary Debate.* Philadelphia: Fortress Press, 1983.

Ska, J.-L. *Il Libro Sigillato e il Libro Aperto.* Biblica. Bologna: EDB, 2005.

Smith, H. P. *A Critical and Exegetical Commentary on the Books of Samuel.* ICC. Edinburgh: T & T Clark, 1912.

Stansell, G. "Honor and Shame in the David Narratives." In *Was ist der Mensch . . . ? Beiträge zur Anthropologie des Alten Testaments. Hans Walter Wolff zum 80. Geburtstag,* edited by F. Crüsemann, C. Hardmeier, and R. Kessler, 94–114. Munich: Kaiser Verlag, 1992.

Stiebert, J., and J. T. Walsh. "Does the Hebrew Bible Have Anything to Say about Homosexuality?" *OTE* 14 (2001): 119–52.

Stone, K. "Gender and Homosexuality in Judges 19, Subject-Honor, Object-Shame?" *JSOT* 67 (1995): 87–107.

Swancutt, D. M. "'The Disease of Effemination': The Charge of Effeminacy and the Verdict of God (Romans 1, 18–2, 16)." In *New Testament Masculinities, Semeia Studies,* edited by S. D. Moore and J. A. Anderson. Society of Biblical Literature, 2003.

Thompson, J. A. "The Significance of the Verb Love in the David-Jonathan Narrative in 1 Samuel." *VT* XXIV (1974): 334–38.

Tonson, P. "Mercy without Covenant: A Literary Analysis of Genesis 19." *JSOT* 95 (2001): 95–116.

Tosato, A. *Il matrimonio. Una teoria generale.* Analecta biblica 100. Rome: Biblical Institute Press, 1982.

———. "I primi richiami di Paolo in tema matrimoniale (1 Ts 4.3–8)." In *Studi sul Vicino Oriente Antico dedicati alla memoria di Luigi Cagni, ed. S. Graziani, Dipartimento di Studi Asiatici,* 1–26. Series Minor 61. Naples: Istituto Universitario Orientale, 2000.

Vermeylen, J. "La maison de Saül et la maison de David." In *Figures de David à travers la Bible,* edited by L. Desrousseaux and J. Vermeylen, 35–74.

Ward, R. B. "Why Unnatural? The Tradition behind Romans 1, 26–27." *Harvard Theological Review* 90 (1997): 263–84.

Wenham, G. J., *Genesis* 1–15. WBC. Waco, TX: Word Books, 1987.

Wénin, A. "David roi, de Goliath à Bethsabée." In *Figures de David à travers la Bible,* edited by L. Desrousseaux and J. Vermeylen, 75–112.

Wink, W. "Homosexuality and the Bible." In *Homosexuality and Christian Faith: Questions of Conscience for the Churches,* edited by W. Wink. Minneapolis: Fortress Press, 1999.

Zehnder, M., "Exegetische Beobachtungen zu den David-Jonathan-Geschichten." *Bib* 79 (1998): 153–79.

General Index

homosexuality and nature, 95–98
homosexual orientation: innate, 94
homosexual practices: negative
    evaluation of, 22–24
hospitality, 12, 18
human action–divine reaction,
    86–88, 98, 99
human impiety, 86

idolatry, 86, 87, 88, 91, 95; and
    homosexual acts, 91
impurity, 87
incest, 54, 55–57, 75

Jesus: beloved disciple, 110–14;
    and the commandment of love,
    115–16; faith of the centurion,
    107–9; fulfillment of the law,
    116–17; Healing of the Slave, 107;
    homosexuality and, 73, 105–6,
    110, 114, 124; and human love,
    114–15, 124; law and mercy, 117–
    22, 124–25; "righteousness" of the
    Pharisee, 119–20
Jewish tradition and Paul, 92
John Chrysostom, 100. *See also
    Homilies on the Letter to the
    Romans*
Jonathan and David, 24–41; in
    context of modern society, 43;
    exchange of armor, 28, 30–31;
    homosexuality and, 29–31, 34, 40–
    41; kissing, 35–37; modification
    of story, 26; overt words and
    gestures, 26–29; parallels between
    Saul's and Jonathan's pursuit of
    David, 38
Josephus, Flavius, 13, 17, 85
Judas, 111

kissing, 35–37

law and mercy, 117–22
Lazarus, 113
lesbianism, 93–94, 96, 123
Letter of Aristeas to Philocratus,
    84–85
Leviticus, Book of: apparent
    contradiction in chap. 20, 64–65;

audience of chap. 18, 60–61; on
    benefits of clear familial relations,
    52–55; on community, 52, 64, 68,
    69–70; on death penalty, 62–65;
    on differences between Israel
    and others, 47–49; formula for
    linking chaps. 18 and 19, 67;
    historical context of chaps. 18
    and 20, 68–69; literary context
    of chaps. 18 and 20, 57–59;
    61–62; on menstruation, 50, 58,
    62, 63, 65; polygamy, 53, 58, 65;
    principal explanations against
    homosexuality, 47–52; prohibition
    against incest, 54; prohibition
    of homosexual relations, 46–47,
    58, 60, 61, 65, 69–70; prohibition
    of homosexual relations in the
    context of incest, 55–57; on
    protection of fertility, 49–50; on
    protection of the extended family,
    50–51; significance of 18:22 and
    20:13 in Biblical theology, 69–71;
    summary conclusions of chaps.
    18–20, 66–68
Life of Abraham. See De Abrahamo
Lord's Prayer, 120–21
Lot, 6, 7, 10–11, 22
lo ta'asu devar hanevalah hazzot, 20
Luke: faith of the centurion, 107–9;
    and slave as object of attention,
    109–10; story of Zacchaeus, 121

malakos and Paul, 73, 74, 76–77,
    78, 79
Mannaseh, 33
Mary, 113
masculorum concubitores, 77–78
Melchisedek, 6
menstruation, 50, 58, 62, 63, 65
mercy and law, 117–22
Michal, 32
Midrash, 30
Milgrom, Jacob, 51n5, 59n10, 64n12
Mishna, 33
modern human society and the
    Bible, 1–2, 42, 43–44
Molech, 58, 60
Mosaic law, 84

mutually consensual homosexuality, 42, 62

Naboth, 62
nature, concept of, 95
nisheq, 35
Nissinen, M., 40
Noah, 6

Paul of Tarsus, 62, 70, 71; argument against homosexuality, 83–89, 98–104; and condemnation of homosexual acts, 104–7, 123; cultural reference of, 92–93; Greco-Roman culture and, 96; on heterosexuals in homosexual relations, 94–95; on homosexual acts and sin, 91; on homosexuality and nature, 95–98, 105–6, 123; on human action–divine reaction, 86–88; on human impiety, 86, 87; on idolatry, 86, 87, 88, 91, 95, 105; interpretations of his writing on homosexuality, 81–82; Jewish tradition and, 92; on lack of respect for the body, 101–3; lists of vices, 74–76, 123; and literary context of Rom. 1:18, 83–86; on loss of freedom, 99–101; moral judgment on homosexual acts, 98–104; mortal blindness, 103–4; Mosaic law and, 84; on passive and active homosexual roles, 76–80; perception of homosexuality, 124; references to Scripture, 88–89, 90–91, 92; theology of creation, 89–92; vision of sexuality, 92; on wickedness, 86. *See also arsenokoitēs* and Paul; *malakos* and Paul; Romans
peace and safety, 50–52
Philo of Alexandria, 13, 76, 85
polygamy, 53, 58, 65
Potiphar, 30
psychological reality of homosexuality, 106, 124, 132

Queen of Sheba, 28
Qumran 4Q51 (4QSam), 25, 32

"righteousness" of the Pharisee, 119–20
Romans, Letter to the: literary context of, 83–86; multiple interpretations regarding homosexuality, 81–83; human action–divine reaction, 86–88. *See also* Paul of Tarsus
rule of life, 45, 51, 57, 69
Ruth, 30

Satan, 100
Saul and David, 27, 30; homosexuality and, 34, 37–38; parallels between Saul and Jonathan, 38; Saul's insult, 31–34
Schenker, Adrien, 3, 123, 127
Septuagint, 25, 32, 92
sexual differentiation, 91, 92
sexual intercourse and new life, 50
Shechem, 27
Sibylline Oracles, 85
sin, 91, 101
sisters and brothers, 53–54
Sodom and Gibeah, parallel texts of, 15, 16–17, 20, 22–24, 41–42
Sodom and Gommorah, 5–13, 51n5; angels and the destruction of Sodom, 7–13; in context of modern society, 42; extrabiblical traditions and, 12–13; general overview of, 9–11; homosexuality and, 20–24; reputation of, 5–7; sins of in other traditions, 12–13
Solomon, 28
Song of Songs, 52
Stoic tradition, 89, 92–93

Talmud of Bablyon, 33
Tamar, 21, 54
Testament of Benjamin, 12
Testament of Levi, 12
Testament of Naphtali, 12
theology of creation, 89–92
Timothy, Letter to: author of, 78–79; Mosaic law, 79
Torah, 46, 47, 70, 71, 123

Zacchaeus, 121

Index of Scriptural Citations

New Testament

Matthew
5–7, 116, 125
9:10, 111
23:23, 121–122

Mark
12:30–31, 115

Luke
7:1–10, 107, 110
7:36–50, 118

John
1:18, 112
6:11, 111
8:1–11, 118
11:8, 121
12:2, 111
13:22–26, 111
13:23, 110
18:15–16, 111
20:2–8, 111
21:22–23, 113

Acts
10:2, 108

Romans
1:18, 83, 84
1:18–32, 73, 80–81, 100, 101, 104
1:19–23, 97
1:23, 86, 95
1:23–27, 91
1:24, 86
1:24–27, 89
1:25, 86, 95
1:26, 95
1:26–27, 93, 98
1:27, 101
1:28, 103
1:32, 103
2, 86
3:20, 83
7:14–20, 100

1 Corinthians
5, 75
5:5, 100
6, 132
6:9, 73, 75, 77, 78, 104, 123
6:9–10, 74

6:12–20, 124
6:20, 102
7, 96, 124, 132
11:3, 97
11:11–12, 97

Ephesians
5, 132

Colossians
3:5, 101

1 Thessalonians
4:3–5, 102

1 Timothy
1:10, 73, 78, 104, 123
1:20, 100

The Bible on the Question of Homosexuality was designed in Walbaum with Museo Slab and typeset by Kachergis Book Design of Pittsboro, North Carolina. It was printed on 60-pound Natures Book Natural and bound by Thomson-Shore of Dexter, Michigan.